Tough Talk
for Tough Times

*Real Conversations for Real People
about Money and Finance*

Money Talks is for everyone. Nancy gives us practical knowledge from her significant experience with her highly successful radio show, her personal life and her professional life. Financial education is learned and this book makes the process doable and enjoyable.

—Pamela P. Smith, Ph.D., President,
Mississippi Council on Economic Education

Having taught personal finance at the college level, I know how complicated and even dull the topic can appear, but Dr. Anderson gets right to the point, in a highly readable style, about money and finance. She brings to print her engaging and insightful manner made popular in her statewide radio program, *Money Talks*. If you wish to understand this vital subject, read this lucid and wise professor and practitioner.

—Lee G. Royce, Ph.D., President, Mississippi College

Tough Talk for Tough Times

Real Conversations for Real People about Money and Finance

Nancy Lottridge Anderson
Ph.D., CFA

QUAIL RIDGE PRESS
BRANDON, MISSISSIPPI

Library of Congress Cataloging-in-Publication Data

Anderson, Nancy Lottridge.
    Tough talk for tough times : real conversations for real people
about money and finance / Nancy Lottridge Anderson.
        p. cm.
    Includes index.
    ISBN-13: 978-1-934193-44-0
    ISBN-10: 1-934193-44-5
1. Finance, Personal. 2. Investments. I. Title.
    HG179.A55973 2009
    332.024--dc22   2009047581

ISBN-13: 978-1-934193-44-0 • ISBN-10: 1-934193-44-5

Design by Cyndi Clark
Printed in the United States of America

First edition, December 2009

QUAIL RIDGE PRESS
P. O. Box 123 • Brandon, MS 39043
info@quailridge.com • www.quailridge.com

Dedication

To Ken. You are my support, my sounding board, and my dearest
friend. Thanks for being a wonderful husband.
And to the other inspirations in my life, my daughter Heather
and her dear husband Kyle.

Acknowledgments

I want to say thank you to my wonderful editor, David G. Miller, Associate Professor of English at Mississippi College. I could only pass on my manuscript knowing he had spent the week grading freshmen essays. His gentle suggestions made this first experience a pleasure. Thank you to my assistant, Lindsey Carpenter, for compiling my many words and chasing down references. Your young eyes and computer skills were invaluable. Another thanks to my other assistant, Jackie Wright, for her insights and ideas. Jackie is invaluable in my daily juggling act.

Thanks to my publicists, Beth Kellogg and Nancy Perkins. It's easy to look organized when you ladies are doing all the work! I also want to thank all my colleagues at Mississippi College School of Business. Dr. Eduardo, you are a jewel! Shea, you brighten each day. In addition, I'd like to thank the folks at Mississippi Public Broadcasting for the opportunity to talk to people each week about money and finance. Ezra, Kevin, and Chris are wonderful on-air partners. Thanks, Sam, for passing on my name to MPB! It's been a fun ride.

Contents

Introduction

The fall of 2008 was the toughest time in my career as bond and stock markets dropped like lead balloons. The near collapse of financial markets changed the world of money management and investing forever. While the problems in the real estate market became evident earlier in the year, few had a clue about the effect on the global economy. The risk taken by companies like AIG and Lehman magnified a difficult situation, leading to the possible collapse of the U.S. financial market.

At first, I found myself echoing the basic principles I learned throughout many finance classes. Later, I was ready to toss out every finance book on my shelf! The game had totally changed. Nothing seemed to help, as the United States faced the biggest financial meltdown since The Great Depression. As 401(k)s plummeted in value, as the real estate market ground to a halt, as jobs dried up like a shallow mud puddle in the Mississippi heat, I listened to the fear in my clients' voices and knew my own brand of fear.

While I tried to stay positive through these tough times, I felt shaken to the core. What had seemed impossible had become very real, and I wondered how this would change the way I manage money. The Financial Meltdown of 2008 had kicked me in the teeth and left me feeling powerless to navigate this new reality.

At my lowest moment, I remembered the basics. As I scrambled to retrieve those finance books from the dumpster, I remembered the wisdom of having a plan and sticking to it. I, also, remembered the wisdom of my frugal parents, both born the year of the Great Stock Market Crash. They taught me the value of a dollar and instilled in me the desire for saving and living sensibly. And I understood that the way to navigate through these tough times was to prepare for the next impossible event.

A couple of years ago, I was approached about doing a call-in radio show about personal finance and investing. At first I thought, "Great, a chance to talk about my favorite subject." My second thought was, "Well, this will run its course in a few months." Once we cover budgeting and basic investing, what else is there? Surely, we'll just find we are repeating ourselves, and the listeners will lose interest. Boy, was I wrong!

Money Talks on Mississippi Public Broadcasting provides listeners with good information and tips on managing their money. While we started with a good audience, that audience became even more attentive after the events of 2008. Suddenly, the topic of money management became crucial to everyone, and I realized the importance of passing on the message of basic financial management—the message taught to me by my parents, my professors, and my life. The program is my soapbox.

Money Talks expands my reach beyond my client base and beyond those students I encounter in the classroom. We have listeners of all ages and all walks of life. Some are just getting started in life while some could teach me a thing or two. It's statewide, with a signal that bleeds into Louisiana, Alabama, and Tennessee.

The panel consists of myself and Chris Burford, a counselor for Consumer Credit Counseling Services. I have twenty years of experience in the investment management business. I am also an Assistant Professor of Finance at Mississippi College. Between the two of us, we cover the broad areas of personal finance and investing. Thankfully, we bring in other experts when we get into the world of taxes or national policy. Kevin Farrell serves as our able moderator.

So, a year and a half later, the program remains popular and we're still talking about money. Sure, sometimes I repeat myself, but that may just be a hazard of my age. People are still listening, and they're still calling in with many of the same questions. When it comes to the complicated world of money and personal finance, repetition is a must. Most of us don't get it the first few times around. We are like the fellow who goes to church every Sunday, listening to the same old sermons, and nodding off halfway through. It's only when we find ourselves in a serious situation that the minister's words take on new meaning. Then, we move to the edges of our seats, hanging on to every word, hoping for some tidbit of wisdom or, at least, some word of grace.

It's the same way with our financial lives. Sure, we hear our parents' speeches. We may have even picked up a book or two on money management. But we never really attend to the message until we find ourselves up against the wall and in a financial mess. Then any talk of money offers the chance for a teachable moment. That's what happened in 2008. People found themselves in difficult situations. They were facing foreclosure. Their credit cards were hitting the limit. Their jobs were in jeopardy. Suddenly, they were ready for a few lessons on financial management.

Every week, the phone lines open, and we talk about money. It's been a very tough year and a half, and the subject couldn't be more important. So, we talk and talk and talk, but the conversation feels like it's just getting started.

CHAPTER ONE

Talking about Talking

Money is a personal issue. In Asian cultures, it's common to ask someone, upon introduction, "How much money do you make?" Such a question in our culture would be considered rude and inappropriate.

My parents are cut from the same Puritan cloth. You are not supposed to talk about how much you make or how much you have in the bank. You live conservatively. You don't display wealth. You live in the same house for forty years, drive your plain vanilla sedan for ten years, and never, ever try to keep up with the Joneses.

They were both born in 1929, the year of the Great Stock Market Crash, and grew up in the lean years of the depression. When I ask them what it was like growing up poor, they look at me with puzzled expressions. Everyone around them was in the same boat, so no one noticed they were poor. There were very few Joneses around with whom to compare their situation.

I think that's what's tough about raising kids today. We truly live in the land of plenty, but there are many grades of plenty within the land. As a result, we spend a lot of time comparing our lives with those around us. When my daughter was growing up, she would tell me about visiting a friend's house. She would say, "Well, you know, they're rich. You should see their house."

TALKING POINT

Don't talk to your children about NOT having money.

Now, I've been in the financial business for over twenty years, so I understand the flaw in this observation. On a regular basis, I see people in my office who live in fine houses and drive fine cars but don't have two cents to rub together. All they have is a pile of bills. I always reminded her that this was no way to judge wealth. In fact, in my experience, it was the folks who lived in simple houses and drove those plain vanilla cars who were more likely to have money.

Many times, I've counseled with a family with grown children. Dad has died, and they are coming with Mom to help sort out her finances. Mom and Dad worked hard at blue-collar jobs. The family lived simply, and Mom still does. When Mom pulls out her portfolio, the children's jaws drop. How did they do it? How did they raise three kids on a middle-class salary and end up with that kind of cash?

I wish I could gather those blue-collar moms and dads in

a room and let them teach the younger generation a thing or two. They are living and breathing testaments to sound financial management. They understand about living within their means, about sacrificing short-term wants for long-term goals, and about finding happiness without securing status symbols.

Strangely enough, people who have grown up with wealth seem unfazed by it. Families who have lived with money for generations don't usually go for ostentatious displays of wealth. But people who have grown up sparingly, while watching their more well-heeled neighbors, can't seem to stay out of money trouble. They have to have the big house and the fine car. They wear the most fashionable labels and sport the finest of everything. They are also heavily in debt. After years of feeling like they are not better than the Joneses, they are determined, by displays of wealth, to show that they are.

That's why I think it's important, in every family, to talk about money. Note I didn't say you should talk about NOT having money. Just talk about money. Talk about the limits of your family's income, but talk about it in a way that conveys gratitude, not deprivation. Teach your children about saving for some cherished item and saving just for the discipline of saving. Teach them that happiness is not attached to material goods, and show them how to be generous with other people.

There are two things about which our attitudes are formed from the time we enter this world. One is sex, and the other is money. I think we are more comfortable talking about our sex lives than we are talking about our financial lives. Allow your daily living to speak loudly and clearly to your children about your attitude about money. Understand that the example your parents set has had a big role in the way you handle money as an adult. I was fortunate. I had a good example. If you didn't, it's not too late, but it is going to take great effort to change those old patterns. You can get an attitude adjustment, but you have to want it—not only for yourself, but for your children. Remember, how you manage your money today will affect how your children manage their own money when they are grown.

Talking about money must be accompanied by your good example and by conscious efforts to find teachable moments with your children. Talk is cheap, but debt is not. So, start talking and keep talking about money issues in your family, and practice what you preach!

Talking to your Spouse

If you are married or in a serious relationship, you need to talk openly about finance. In every couple, gifts and inclinations are different. One person likes to keep track of the money, while the other is haphazard about money. It's only natural that one person will take charge of the finances, but that doesn't mean the other one can abdicate and play the ignorant role. Both should be on the same page when it comes to money.

Statistically, women are more likely to take care of the day to day budgetary items.[1] They handle buying the kids' clothes and the groceries. They may take care of the regular monthly bills. Men are more likely to make the long-term investment decisions. They set up retirement accounts and college funds and choose the stocks and mutual funds. But every couple is different.

---

1 The Buzz, *Money Magazine*.

My mother always took care of the money, and I do it for my family. I pay the bills AND make the investment decisions, but that's also my job. It's a natural fit for me to take care of these things at home, as well as at the office. My husband trusts my judgment, but that doesn't mean he should be out of the loop. While I handle the bill-paying, he balances the check-book. That way, we both see what goes in and out of the household account. No ONE person

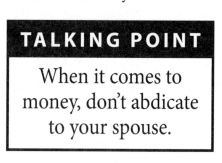

TALKING POINT

When it comes to money, don't abdicate to your spouse.

has total control. There are no secrets when it comes to the money. We talk often about money issues and what our short-term and long-term goals are.

I still see too many women who are totally ignorant about their family's finances. They have given over control to their husbands, and they choose to stay in the dark about money. I am puzzled by this since part of being an adult is learning to manage your money. What happens to these women when their husbands leave or die? When my own daughter got married, I told her, "Don't abdicate. It may be easier to sit back and allow your husband to handle this aspect of your life, but it's not smart."

Each couple must also decide how to handle individual earned income, household bills, and discretionary items. When a couple walks in my door, I ask them to tell me how they handle money. I don't dispense advice on how to do it. I've learned that every couple is different. Some like to maintain totally separate accounts. Some are comfortable with everything being in joint accounts. I don't pass judgment on the method. I just say, "Hey, whatever works." What I do encourage is talk.

BEFORE you get married, discuss your expectations for money. Talk about the patterns set in your families. Talk, talk, and talk some more about this important issue. Then, when you marry, you will find that you still didn't talk enough. You will be surprised by your spouse's approach and attitude to money. So, you must keep talking about money issues, and you must learn to adapt and find a way that works for your family.

If you find yourselves in a financial mess, don't avoid the subject. Decide, as a couple, to address the problem head on. Get help from an independent advisor if you need to. Just having an objective voice is often helpful. Men need to understand that, for women, money is about security. We need to feel safe. Women need to understand that, for men, money is about strength and trust. They need to feel that women trust them to handle things. These two goals are often in conflict. If you can't get past this, get outside help.

Before you bring children into the world, the two of you need to be on the same page financially. If you can't manage your money when it's just you two, boy, are you going to have trouble when the children arrive! The financial demands of rearing children are tremendous. In addition, you need to present the same attitude and values about money to your children as they grow. So, talk to each other first, so you can be prepared to talk to your children later.

Talking to Preschoolers

It's never too early to talk to your children about money, but, just like the sex talk, you need to do this gradually, editing your speech for their age and maturity. With preschoolers, money talks should center around the concrete and literal. The trick for modern parents will be to keep cash (dollar bills and coins) on them. In this society of debit and credit cards, you lose out on opportunities for good financial lessons.

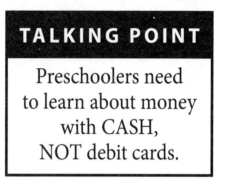

TALKING POINT

Preschoolers need to learn about money with CASH, NOT debit cards.

Imagine the four year old accompanying Mom to the grocery store. As far as he knows, you only need a bit of plastic to buy food. So, what's the problem with using the plastic to buy that extra bag of candy? And you only need one swipe of the card to buy both a little and a lot. How confusing for that four year old!

You probably won't take cash for your weekly grocery trip, but you can give your child cash for his purchases. Yes, I'm a believer in allowances. I also believe the money should be tied to work. After all, that's what we all face in the real world. Make sure the chores and the allowance fit their age.

Allowing a child to purchase items for himself does two things. It gives him some control over his world and shows him that life is about choices. If you only have $1, you have to choose between the Twix candy bar and the Three Musketeers. You can't have both. As a parent, you still have the right to limit those choices, but don't choose for him. Have you ever watched a four year old standing before the candy counter trying to choose? You can see the wheels turning. You can sense the angst of a major decision. It's a painstaking, beautiful moment. Ahh, and the relief and pure joy when the purchase is finally made. How sweet it is!

Making your own money and learning how to spend it are lessons that should come early and often. Children should learn to see it as both precious and common. It's precious because you must earn it. It's common because we must use it every day to buy the things we need.

Young children need to handle money. I know. I know. It's pretty dirty stuff, but then, so are kids! I'm from the school of "a little dirt never hurt anybody." Get them used to the denominations—dollar bills, quarters, dimes, nickels. Help them count out their money. It's a great way to get them started with math. Get them a wallet or change purse to carry their earnings. If they lose it, don't cave and replenish their coins. You're just teaching them that, when it comes to money, there's a bottomless pit. The pain of the loss will be minimal, but the lesson will last a long time.

Teach them to save. Get them a piggybank. Encourage (don't force) them to put a portion of their allowance into their bank. Ask them if there is some toy they would like to save for. Write the amount of the toy on a chalkboard. Keep up with their savings. When they get to the magic number, break into the bank and head to the store.

Teach them to be generous. Encourage (again, don't force) them to use a portion of their allowance for some good cause. If you attend church, have them put money in the offering plate. You could have them save for a special donation to another organization. Children are concrete, so they may want to save for a toy for a friend. For this money, it doesn't matter what they spend it on, as long as they don't spend it on themselves. You will give them the joy of charitable giving, and it will last a lifetime.

Don't burden them with serious family problems. You won't be able to hide that you've lost your job, but you can reassure them that they will be cared for and the family will be fine. Don't discuss credit problems in front of them. They won't understand it, but they'll sense something is wrong. If you face home foreclosure, try to explain the limits of your income. Try to be upbeat about your new living situation. At this age, children need security and stability. Moving will be traumatic. Suck it up, and put a good face on it for them.

And, if you go through a divorce, keep alimony, child support, etc. to yourself. Don't bad-mouth your ex over money. Don't discuss money issues with your ex within your children's earshot. Don't make your children ask your ex for money. Be the adult. Money issues between divorced spouses DON'T need to be talked about when the kids are around. Don't connect money to love or relationship in any way. Money is just what we use to get the things we need to live every day.

Talking to Grade School Children

As your children get older, the chores AND the allowance should grow with them. You'll be there to cover the big things, like piano lessons and camp, but let them use their money for the trip to the skating rink or to the movie. Again, you can limit their choices but always allow them to choose how they spend their money.

TALKING POINT

Teach grade school children about charity.

Encourage them to save for longer periods of time for even bigger items. Delaying a purchase helps to build discipline. It forces them to look carefully at the object of their desire. They may decide, after a few weeks, that it's not worth the wait. Or they may really want it. Anticipating the purchase is sweet, because when you finally get that Playstation, it's just the best. They are less likely to toss it aside when it's their money and when they've had to save patiently for it.

If you've started saving for their college (and I hope you have by now), show them the statement. You may have chosen a 529 plan that is invested in mutual funds. They won't understand it, but they'll know you're saving and investing for something that is far in the future.

You're introducing them to the idea of investing, and you're planting the seed for college. They won't really be ready to learn about stocks and mutual funds for a few years yet (unless you have a Warren Buffett on your hands), but they'll become familiar with the idea. Here again, the idea is to make money both precious and common, not something foreign and confusing.

Encourage them to save for family Christmas gifts, as well as other gifts. They won't be able to purchase much, but it will be more meaningful for them AND for the recipient. Encourage them to assist in a fund raiser for a group— girl scouts, for instance. They will learn to work with a group to raise money for a good cause. They will then enjoy the collective joy of charitable giving.

Talking to Teenagers

This is where it gets hard. Teenagers think they are grown. We know they're not. The trick is to play along with their delusion, while keeping a firm grip on the reins. This is a good time for them to get a real job. Giving them an allowance for chores helps connect money to work, but when Mom and Dad are still the boss, it makes for a touchy situation.

They need to have the experience of a taskmaster that is not related to them and invested in them. They need an objective person telling them what to do. Teenagers can't abide their parents telling them what to do. They roll their eyes. They complain. They whine. We understand that being an adult doesn't mean you get to do everything you want. Adults still have to follow rules and orders. Your teen needs to understand that money comes with strings. The folks with the cash get to tell you what to do. If you don't want to do it, fine, but you also forego the cash.

In the early teens, the work may be babysitting or mowing lawns. Encourage them to set up a formal business, with a business bank account. Show them how to track their income and expenses. Teach them to create their own invoices and business cards. Help them with a marketing plan. This can be as simple as copying fliers to distribute. This is the time to learn about basic business principles.

When they get a little older, they'll be ready to look for a job with an employer. Help them develop a resume. It can be very simple. Also, help them come up with a list of potential employers. I think it's such a great experience to walk into a strange workplace, hat in hand, and ask for a job. Explain that rejection is not personal.

When they get that first paycheck, show them the difference between gross income and net income. Now is a good time to get used to taxes. Encourage them (but don't insist) to save a portion of each check. This is a good time to set up a Roth IRA for your child. All they need to have is earned income in order to qualify. They may grumble now, but they'll thank you in twenty years.

The most important thing you can do for teenagers, when it comes to money, is to let them do without. That doesn't mean they have to go hungry or wear tattered jeans—oh yeah, they already do that! It means that you give them a reason to work. Don't just hand them cash every time they ask. Expect them to live within their means—whatever you have set that up to be. If they spend all their money three days before the next paycheck or allowance, don't cave and give them more. Let them sit at home while their friends go to the movie. Let them leave their car parked because of an empty gas tank. This is SO hard to do! Believe me, I know. I've caved plenty, and I've regretted it each time.

If you can do this, you'll be amazed at the result. Those innovative, ingenious creatures will find a way. Suddenly, they'll be offering to wash your car. They'll be digging in the couch for change. They'll be offering their services to strangers. Deprivation is motivating.

Don't expect them to step up on their own. They are human beings, and we humans only do what we have to do. If someone is willing to pay your bills and give you all the money you need, why would you ever budge off the couch? That would be stupid! Our job, as parents, is to push them, sometimes kicking and screaming, into adulthood.

During the junior high years, shopping for clothes with my

daughter was a nightmare. It was a constant fight with her demanding everything she saw and my holding the line on the budget. I decided to try a new tactic. I gave her a clothing budget. It was a generous budget, and it had only one constraint. Anything she picked out must be modest. All the important parts had to be covered! Beyond that, she was only limited by the budget limit.

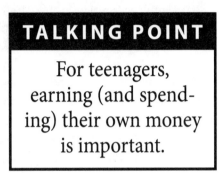

TALKING POINT

For teenagers, earning (and spending) their own money is important.

She was thrilled! And off we went to the mall. I loved it because it took all the pressure off me. She loved it because she got to have control and make decisions about her own clothes. Perfect, right? Well, not exactly. She got carried away, even though I kept reminding her where she stood on her spending. When she hit the limit, I calmly announced, "You're done."

She was shocked. After all, she had so many other things on her list she had planned to buy. How could she have spent all that money? Then, she began to sob. As she was having a meltdown in the store, I just calmly paid the bill. The salesclerk was a little puzzled by the whole event.

What a great lesson this was—for both of us. My daughter learned about the limits of money and about making choices. I learned that a tug of war with a teenager can be avoided if you give them some control over their own lives. They're just trying to grow up. Let them!

During the teen years is also a good time to set up a bank account. Let them have a debit card. My daughter had her first bank account in high school, complete with that card. She loved it! She thought the ATM machine magically gave her money. She came home one day telling about going through the bank drive-thru for cash. The machine wouldn't give her money. Of course, she was outraged. She parked the car, and marched up to the teller, demanding to know what the problem was. The teller told her she only had $6.32 in her account. Her response? Oh.

DON'T put overdraft protection on that teenager's account. You heard me. If you want to teach them about living within their means, let them bounce a few checks. I lost count of the number of overdraft notices that showed up in our mailbox. It took repeated instances, but my duaghter finally got it when she realized her afternoon shopping spree had been nixed by overdraft charges. It's a powerful and humbling lesson to face an overdraft notice and one that every teenager needs. Let it happen now, while you're there to help sort it out. Pulling stunts like that as an adult isn't fun.

This is also a good time to start teaching them about investments. If you don't know anything, get a book! Learn about mutual funds and stocks and bonds. Pass on that knowledge to them. A great way to teach them about stocks is to let them pick a company that they are familiar with. They'll learn about the connection between company earnings and shareholder return. Show them how to open a mutual fund or brokerage account. These days, everything can be done online, and kids take to this like crazy.

In Mississippi, we encourage participation in the stock market game in our schools. These investment teams usually put professionals to shame. Teaching them how to make money grow is an invaluable lesson. Earning money is important, but getting your money to earn money is the real key to wealth. Kids who learn about investing at this age will be lifelong investors. It's how Warren Buffett got started!

Talking to College Students

By the time your child heads to college, you should have laid the groundwork for sound financial management. Despite all your efforts, though, they may go crazy. After all, for many, it's the first time away from Mom and Dad. Expect them to make a few mistakes along the way. Hopefully, they will be errors that can be fixed.

You should already have a bank account set up. Use this account to funnel money to your children to cover expenses in college. Tuition and room and board will be spelled out up front. Make deposits into his account for this purpose, and let him actually pay

TALKING POINT

Put your college student on a tight budget. Too much disposable income for them spells trouble.

the bill. He'll be more aware of your sacrifice in sending him to school, but he'll also feel like the adult paying his own way.

If you pursue scholarships or loans, have your student participate in the process. Get him to fill out forms and conduct searches. Explain the paperwork and loan statements to him. You will serve as translator for all the financial jargon, and you will be teaching him the language of money.

Before he heads for campus, set up a budget for all other expenses—like food. That's the big one, especially if you have boys. Deposit money into his account, per this budget, on a regular basis. You may start with doing this once a week, but move to fewer monthly deposits with larger amounts. A deposit every two weeks is more like what he can expect when he starts to draw a paycheck. If he gets to the end of week one and is broke, hold the line. I know you don't want them to starve, but if they have a meal plan, they won't. They'll mope. They'll pout, but they'll learn to pace themselves when it comes to money.

Set up his budget so that it covers the necessities, but leaves little for anything else. This is called motivation. He will probably start thinking about a part-time job to cover all the extras. This is a good thing. College students can easily handle a full-time load at school and a part-time job. It may cut into their partying time, but you are getting them ready for the real world.

Expect them to work during the summer. In fact, the best thing you can do is cut them off during the summer months. Again, we are looking for motivation. You don't need to nag and threaten. You just need to zip up your wallet and hold the line. They'll come around.

Talking to Young Adults

Make it clear to your young adults when the gravy train stops. For many, this should be at graduation. Turn over the cell phone bill, the insurance bill, and any other regular bills you've been covering. Have a clear cut-off. Don't let it drag out.

Do this even if their job situation is not the best. They may have a degree, but they can't find a job. Still, they need to take responsibility for themselves. They may even move back in with you. We are hearing more and more about grown children moving back in with their parents because of financial reasons. You can help them without being a crutch by having them cover some of the household expenses. This can be done reasonably. Remember, the goal is to get them out and on their own. My personal testimony is that the empty nest is great!

> **TALKING POINT**
>
> Have a definite timeline for cutting off adult children.

When they get that first job, ask them if they have a retirement plan at work. Help them read through the paperwork. Encourage them to start contributing as soon as possible. And encourage them to continue their education in the world of investing. They will need this as that 401(k) grows.

Hopefully, you have been talking a lot about money by now. That means your children know your values, as it relates to finances, and they know you as a good source of information. They may call you when it comes time to buy that first house. Be ready to answer questions. Feel free to offer tips and tricks, but stay at arm's length and let them be independent adults, because, now, you can finally stop talking!

Talking about Grace

Now, while I am doling out advice about teaching money to children, let me say that I've made every mistake in the book.

Some children have a natural affinity for managing their money. My daughter was not one of those. In fact, I have said, many times, that if it weren't for the fact that she looks just like me, I'd say she was swapped at the hospital!

That means that each lesson about money came with great difficulty. Usually, it took several events before it sunk in with her. It also means that I learned from doing, and you will, too. I've also learned from other parents. I've listened to their stories and found some tricks along the way to rearing money savvy children. And every kid is different. So, try things. Adjust when you need to. And for goodness sake, talk to other parents.

> **TALKING POINT**
>
> Allow your children to "mess up," but don't allow them to avoid the consequences.

In some cases, you need to band together to fend off the attacks from your children. I'll pass along four rules given to me by "Bill from Brandon," one of our callers on the show.

Rule Number 1: Don't let your "wanter" exceed your "getter."

Rule Number 2: The sooner you learn that it doesn't hurt to want, the better off you'll be.

Rule Number 3: Remember the Rule of 72. Take your interest earned and divide it into 72. This tells you how many years it will take to double your money.

Rule Number 4: Remember your ratio. Figures don't lie, but liars figure. Don't spend over 38% of your take-home pay for any indebtedness over 6 months.

Wise words from "Bill."

You will make mistakes along the way. Bestow grace on your children and give yourself a little grace, as well. Know that teaching them about money is one of the most important things you can do. So, start talking about it in the right way when they first come into the world. Keep talking about it to educate them about choices and control. Most importantly, talk loudly and clearly by setting a good example in your own life.

CHAPTER TWO

Talking about Spending Plans

Getting Rid of a Dirty Word

My co-host Chris Burford likes to soften his words when he talks about budgeting. He says, "Don't call it a budget. Call it a spending plan." Budgeting has such a negative image. We usually think of it as drudgery, something that points out our failures and makes us feel deprived. "Spending plan" has a much nicer ring to it. And that's what it is. We are planning how to spend our money, rather than being haphazard with those expenditures.

While I agree with the choice of language, I still find most families have a hard time putting this into practice. Setting up a budget is easy, but living by it is another thing all together. Who has time to keep up with every receipt and track it with your spending plan? After all, we are busy trying to get the kids to school and soccer, working two jobs, and trying to find time to take care of yard and housework. Who does this?

The truth is some people enjoy keeping financial records and budgets. They are accountants and engineers who love order and numbers and would rather spend time tracking expenses than having an intimate conversation about the meaning of life. Their lives are ordered by spreadsheets and financial programs, and they enjoy the process of budgeting.

I have watched many families, full of good intentions, set up budgets and begin the process of living by their plans. Most usually make it about six months. After that, the receipts pile up. The spreadsheet goes untouched. Life gets hectic, and they just give up. I can speak from experience. I started out so well but became overwhelmed by the process. I felt as if I needed a full-time clerk to keep up with everything. Budgeting has a bad reputation. The word causes many people to run in the other direction, not even giving it a try. For the rest of us, our experience with budgeting has left a bad taste in our mouths.

Is there another approach? One that can help us control our spending without creating more work and anxiety? What can most normal people do to help them with a spending plan—one, they can develop and live by for years?

Budgeting Crazy

I recommend an alternative approach. Don't try to live on a budget or spending plan for everything. Instead, concentrate on the areas I call your "insanities." You could call this budgeting for your crazy moments.

We all have them. It's that one area of our lives where temptation and impetuousness take over. You throw caution to the wind, and spend like there's no tomorrow, but only when it comes to this one area of your life. Normally, you're sane. You know how much money you need to pay your bills. You tell yourself, "No, I really don't need that," and you walk away. But when it comes to that ONE thing, your eyes glaze over. You forget about the bills. Before you know it, you've whipped out the credit card and shouted, "What the heck! You only live once."

Now, I don't know what that is for you. Maybe, it's your children. Those sweet little eyes are looking up at you, and you don't want to deny them anything. Maybe, it's your dog. Before you know it, you've booked weekly massages for Fifi to help with her stress over the new cat. Maybe, it's clothes. You just need the latest, greatest fashion item. Maybe, it's woodworking tools, or books, or travel, or. . . . The list is endless.

For a married couple, crazy comes in twos. Your husband loves old cars. You love gardening. Coming up with a plan to control both can save your relationship. It gives each of you the control and freedom to enjoy the things you love while not putting your family in a precarious financial situation. It's just an agreed upon cap for those few expenses that get you into trouble.

The trick is to know yourself and know your insanity. As a family, sit down and address the insanity. This is not a time for recriminations. After all, when you work hard, you want to be able to enjoy some of the fruits of your labor. Your spending plan should not try to eliminate your insanity, only control it. If you can figure out what this crazy spot is and plan and monitor it, you'll be fine. You won't need to budget for everything else on a regular basis. You just need to keep up with and keep in check the crazy!

The Starting Point

To start this process, you have to begin the old-fashioned way. Sorry, but there's no way around the drudgery, but you'll only need to do this once. Develop an initial spending plan that takes into account all your expenditures. A good way to do this is to go back through your checking account for at least six months. You may need to back up an entire year. You want to come up with a monthly amount for each item.

Some people love computer spreadsheets. Some people prefer paper and pencil. It doesn't matter how you do it. Just get the numbers down. Remember, you won't need to do this every month. The first time can be daunting as you really look at where your money is going.

Once you develop an overall spending plan, you should be able to put it in a drawer. You only need to revisit it about once a year. But if something big happens, you will need to pull it out and dust it off. The big things could be the loss of a job, an impending wedding, or a major illness. Otherwise, things should stay the same, and you can stay on course, as long as you reign in your crazy.

Some things occur each and every month. Every month, you pay your mortgage/rent, electric bill, phone bill, etc. Some bills, like your mortgage or the gym membership, are the same each month. That's easy. Some fluctuate. Electric bills don't usually stay the same, except in the case of forcing them to.

By the way, I don't recommend this. Fluctuating electric bills remind us to turn off the lights and adjust the thermostat. You'll need to come up with an average amount for each of these fluctuating bills. Aim on the high side. It's better to be surprised by being over prepared than to be caught short.

Don't forget those bills that occur fewer than twelve times a year. Car insurance usually is paid every six months. Other insurance may occur quarterly. Some bills only pop up once a year. Make sure you account for every expenditure you may face during the year. Divide those annual bills by twelve to get the monthly amount you'll need to cover the payment.

One of your biggest bills will be groceries. Looking at this expense over a six month period will give you a good idea of your typical monthly bill. Account for everything in your account by allotting it to an expense account. Then, put in a pad for miscellaneous, because, when it comes to life, the unexpected is the norm. I'm the girl scout at my house, so I prefer to be prepared for the unexpected.

Split out your credit card bills. List amounts spent on each type of expense, like clothes or travel or health care. This may get tricky when you don't pay off your bill each month. You'll need to look at your statement and estimate costs for each.

Now, compare your total monthly expenses with your total take-home pay. If the outgo is bigger than the income, you'll need to start cutting. Later, we'll also talk about budgeting for saving because that is an important part of any budget. For right now, you just need to have a spending plan that amounts to less than your income. As you look over your newly prepared spending plan, what is that one discretionary account that sticks out? That's the place you need to cut, and that's the place you need to apply some discipline.

Controlling the Crazies

Each family needs to understand that first, the regular bills must be paid. We should know what the figure is to cover those regular bills. It should be imprinted on our foreheads. What gets us into trouble is the crazy stuff. Let's suppose that, when all the regular stuff is paid, you have $200 left. Your husband's "crazy" is his workshop. He just loves tools! Go figure. Your "crazy" is shoes. No explanation needed!

You both sit down and decide that you can each spend $100 per month on your crazy. Of course, he'll say, "What kind of tool can I get for $100?" And you'll say, "I saw a screwdriver for $19.99. But I love Manolo Blahnik's." No explanation needed!

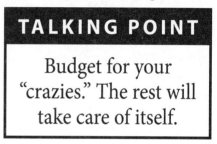

TALKING POINT

Budget for your "crazies." The rest will take care of itself.

So, now you have a spending plan where no one gets what he wants... at least, in the short-run. You have to save up for anything more than $100. If he wants a $500 tool (God only knows why!), then he must save his crazy for five months to make the purchase. And if you want a $400 pair of shoes, you must save for four months. If you agree on a monthly amount for these items, it's just a matter of staying within those limits.

For most people, this is an easier approach to take when it comes to budgeting. It means you don't have to track EVERY expense, only those few where you get a little nutty. As long as you keep your hands off bill-paying money and set aside money for savings, the rest is easy. In fact, this tool can give you a way to say no. Just when you're ready to buy that second pair of red shoes (not that I would do that), you check your budget and realize you're short $50. The voice of reason pops into your head. You put down the shoes. You put away your credit card, and you back slowly away from the cash register. When the cool breeze hits your face as you walk out of the store, sanity will return. I promise!

Have a way to keep yourself accountable. If you're married, verify to your spouse that you are staying within budget on those items. If you're single, it's a little harder, but be honest with yourself. Keep a record, whether on paper or on computer, of the crazy stuff. If you blow it one month by spending $1000, then you'll need to sacrifice for several months, until your spending plan catches up to your actual expenditures.

So, forget about spending hours each month tracking expenses on a ledger or a spreadsheet. Spend a Saturday afternoon getting your financial life on paper. After that, you can hone in on your crazy spot, and set a spending limit. Be disciplined in this one area, and everything else should take care of itself.

One last word of caution… tomorrow's crazy hasn't shown up yet. Be aware of changing interests and changing spending habits. Tomorrow, your husband may give up woodworking and decide he is into old cars. If that happens, just transfer the limits to the new crazy, because when it comes to money, there's only one kind of crazy.

CHAPTER THREE

Talking about Credit Cards

P sst… I want to whisper something in your ear.

The secret to building wealth lies in the ability to control consumer debt. Consumer debt occurs when we use our credit cards. Average credit card debt in the United States now stands at about $10,000 per family[1]. That's astonishing.

How do you rack up that kind of debt on a credit card? Well, it happens one small purchase at the time. For some, it's frivolous, impulsive spending that does it. For others, it happens because of big life events—a job loss, a divorce, an illness. Regardless, it happens. When I meet with people who find themselves "in the ditch," it's not my job to lecture them on

---

1 "The truth about credit card debt," *MSN Money.*

TALKING POINT

You want to get rich? Get a handle on that consumer debt!

their excessive spending or make them feel bad about a financial crisis. My job is to help them get out of the ditch, and you can't get out of the ditch by digging a deeper hole! You MUST stop spending, and it must be a family decision to change your lifestyle.

Back to that secret, I promise you that if you take control of this one area of your money, you'll be amazed. You will have all that you need to live, and you'll end up with extra each month. Years of this practice will mean a higher standard of living. Show me two families with identical incomes. One has that average debt on the credit card. One does not. The one without the debt is living large—nice vacations, good schools for the kids, nice homes, and comfortable retirement. There is a big payoff for practicing restraint when it comes to the plastic. So, repeat after me: The secret to happiness and fortune is to be the master of your credit card instead of being the slave to your MasterCard.

The Big Goal

Now, let's talk about the BIG GOAL. The BIG GOAL is to pay off your credit card balance each and every month. That means that you never make a purchase unless you know you'll have money in your account to cover the bill when it arrives. So why would a person like that need a credit card? A credit card is a convenience. In fact, in our society, it's difficult NOT to have a card. You can't purchase things over the phone or online without one. It's certainly faster at the gas pumps and at the cash register. It can help you track expenditures. It gives mothers peace of mind when their children travel. Credit cards, in and of themselves, are not evil. And while we humans have a tendency to abuse our cards, we have the ability to control those tendencies.

Everyone has experienced the "sneak up on you" card statement. You haven't had any huge expenses during the month. It's just been a little here and a little there. And then the statement arrives, and you can't believe how much you've charged. You're certain there's been a mistake, so you check on every charge. You add and read, and you find that, yes, you DID do all that damage.

Find a way to track your monthly charges. Some people tape their receipts to the fridge or to the mirror. Some like to record them in a ledger or in a computer program. You may want to put a running total in your phone note pad.

TALKING POINT

When it comes to credit cards, the BIG GOAL is to pay off the balance each month.

Your system doesn't have to be complicated or even very organized. It just needs to remind you how this amount is accumulating. Having those numbers in front of your nose will make you think twice about that additional purchase.

Next, know the total amount that you can afford each month on your card. That goes back to your spending plan. Make sure that all your necessities are covered, and you aren't dipping into that money for that cute pair of shoes or the tickets to the baseball game. Keep your charging within your allotted amount and keep up with those receipts. Don't let your credit card statement sneak up on you.

Never, EVER put necessities on the charge card. Don't use it at the grocery store. Don't use it to pay your car note. And never use it to pay your taxes. For those items, stick with checks and debit cards. Necessities will keep popping up, so using plastic for these items is a recipe for a credit mess. You'll just keep coming back to the card each month, and you'll hit that $10,000 average in no time.

TALKING POINT

You only need ONE credit card!

Reaching the big goal requires discipline. You must decide to put off your "wants" and sacrifice short-term pleasure. While discipline sounds boring and a drudgery, bear in mind the end result. It's like dieting or exercise. Doing without chocolate cake or running a mile a day sounds like a drudge until you view your fit, slim body a few months later. In fact, it's even better than that. At my age, I know that regular exercise and watching my diet is now part of my lifestyle. With financial discipline, there is the wonderful "carrot" that comes after years of restraint. Sacrificing now means you'll have money to burn later on. A diet that forces me to give up chocolate cake for a year so that I could eat all the chocolate cake I want later would be my dream! That's the kind of financial diet I'm recommending. Whenever you are tempted to over consume, remember the incredible banquet you'll feast on later

One Big Statement

Now, I'm going to shout.

YOU ONLY NEED ONE CREDIT CARD!

You don't need six different cards. You don't need store credit cards. You don't need gasoline credit cards. You just need one all around card—a Visa or MasterCard will do the trick. They are accepted everywhere, so there should be no problem when you hit the stores. They are accepted across the globe, so you don't need anything else when you travel.

One card means one big statement. Everything that you have purchased on credit shows up on one statement. That one dollar amount will hit you in the face full force. So many people fool themselves into thinking they don't have a credit issue. In fact, they have no idea of the total amount outstanding on their cards. The statements trickle in, each with reasonable amounts outstanding, each with a different interest rate. Whenever I work with someone struggling with credit issues, the first thing we do is to list each card, its outstanding balance, and its interest rate. Then I add up the total. That's when I hear the gasp.

Credit card companies want us to be foolish. That's how they make money—big money. I confess that I have been enticed by the "10% off today's purchase if you open an account." In the past, I've been diligent about closing them as soon as I get that first bill. But I'm getting old and addled, and my life is busy. I forget to close them out. I forget the cards are still circulating. And, the credit card companies have made it really difficult to close an account. If you try to do it online, it's like finding a needle in a haystack. If you try to do it on the phone, make sure you carve out an afternoon of going through multiple menus and listening to elevator music while on hold. It's just not worth it to me anymore. Remember, they just want to get you buy more stuff and let it sit on that card so they can earn more interest. They count on us being forgetful and undisciplined.

So, my new resolution is to "just say no" when that salesperson offers me a discount for a store card. It takes every ounce of resolve to go against my bargain-hunting nature, but I know it's not worth the hassle. Forget the deals. It's just a trick to get you to play the fool.

One card. One statement. One set of interest rates. It's simple. It's easy. And yes, it's painfully honest, but feeling a little pinch, when it comes to credit, is a good thing. If your family manages its budget from a joint account, one account is enough, with each member having his own card. My husband and I maintain separate cards, just because they are holdovers from our single days. If you manage your household budget with separate accounts, each member may want to have a separate card to easily keep up with purchases. And, of course, if you have a business, keep those purchases on a separate card. Otherwise, one is really enough.

Don't get enticed by discounts. Don't get fooled by pre-approved offers. Shred the junk mail. Delete the e-mails. Ignore the sales clerk. Repeat after me: One big statement.

Getting Out of the Ditch

But what if you are already in trouble? So, you've made a mess. You're up to your neck in credit card debt, spending way too much of your monthly income just covering the minimum payments. Talking about credit cards does NOT need to turn into a lecture at this point. You just need help getting out of the ditch.

TALKING POINT

It may have been easy getting into debt, but it's going to be HARD work getting out.

The approach is simple. It's nothing new. You may need to find a few new tricks to get yourself to stay on track. More than anything, you need to find the determination to break a bad habit. It won't be easy. Depending on how big the mess is, it could take anywhere from one to three years to dig out, but it's worth the effort. Freedom from the weight of all that credit dirt is amazing.

Start by listing each card, its outstanding balance, its required minimum payment, and its interest charge. If you're a computer person, set it up on a spreadsheet. If you like pencil and paper, record these on a ledger pad. Each month will have a separate column showing the checks you'll write and how the balances will decline over the months (hopefully).

Add up the monthly minimums on all the cards. Now, comes the hard part. Look at your spending plan. After you've paid the regular bills like the house note, the car note, groceries, utilities, etc., what's left from your monthly income? Don't include the credit card payments in the regular bills. They are separate.

Make sure you've accounted for all the regular expenses. Don't forget those once a quarter or once a year items like car insurance. Always put in a little "pad" I call miscellaneous. The amount that's left over will be what you'll apply to credit card debt each month until your debt is paid off.

Here's an example:

Monthly Take Home Pay
(what you actually put into your checking account): $3000
Monthly Regular Expenses:

House Note	$1000
Utilities	$ 200
Groceries	$ 400
Car Note	$ 500
Misc.	$ 400
Net Left Over for Credit Cards	$ 500

What if the amount left over equals the minimum payments? Then, you've got trouble. You'll never get out of the ditch if you can't pay more than the minimum required. You have to be able to shovel larger amounts in their direction to get the credit card companies off your back. You only have a couple of options. One is to look for pennies wherever you can find them. Cut back your expenses. Can you live without cable for a while? Can you cut your utility bill? Can you lower your cell phone expenses? Can you cut your grocery bill? Look for frivolous items, like the gym membership you never use or the magazine subscription that you never read. To make this work, you may have to tighten your belt to find the dollars you need. Sit down as a family and discuss the need for sacrifice. Enlist everyone's help. Make it a game, with the reward coming after the big payoff.

What if it's still not enough? One option would be to use equity in your house to deal with the credit. I don't usually like to recommend this, but sometimes, there's no other good option. Putting credit card debt on your house means you could lose the house if you don't make the payment. That's where the danger lies. Choose this option as a last resort, and resolve to never go back to your old ways. This requires dealing with your bank or mortgage company. You could use a home equity line of credit, or you could do a cash-out refinance. Be upfront with your lender about your reasons for doing this. They will see this on your credit history, anyway. Most will require that checks be made out to the credit card companies. They want to make sure you are really clearing out those cards.

Remember, though, we are in tough credit times. You may find no one willing to give you the money to do this. If this happens, and there is no way for you to cut your expenses to do it on your own, there may be only one thing left—bankruptcy. Bankruptcy does not carry the stigma that it used to, but it's still not painless. Before you take this drastic step, consult with a financial advisor and a bankruptcy attorney. Know what you're getting into. Make sure this is the only option open to you.

But bankruptcy is only the extreme solution. What if you are not facing that? You have $500 a month you KNOW you can apply to credit card debt. Suppose your minimum payments add up to $300. Now, you're ready to complete your spreadsheet or ledger.

I shop by looking at the price tag. The cheaper something is, the more inclined I am to like it! Everyone knows how to shop for shoes or groceries or televisions. You check the price tag. But do you know how to shop for money? Just do it the same way. Check the price tag!

Huh?

The price of money is the interest you pay to borrow the money. Think of that interest charge as the price tag. Lower interest charges cost you less than higher interest charges. And since I'm a bargain shopper, I LOVE cheap money!

Fill in each month for each card with the minimum amount. With your extra $200, go back and find the most expensive money. That will be the card with the highest interest charge. Put that extra money on that puppy and keep doing it till the debt is gone. Month after month after month. When it disappears, you'll not only have that $200, but you'll have the minimum amount from that card, to put on the next most expensive card. Let's suppose that is $75 plus $200, so you can add $275 to the next card down the line. Pay the extra on that card month after month after month until it disappears. Just keep doing that until all the debt is gone. Simple.

Find a way to celebrate the disappearance of each card. You can use smiley face stamps or star stickers. Invite the family to join in a wild dance to the tune of "Money, Money, Money." Seeing that list shrink is priceless.

For many, this will be a long-term process. I remember worrying over my post-baby weight after I had my daughter. Someone reminded me that it took 9 months to gain it. I needed to give myself at least 9 months to get rid of it. Your credit worries didn't happen overnight. Expect to spend time and effort to get out from under that debt.

While you are marking off those cards, you have to commit to living on a cash basis. The stronger this commitment, the shorter your time of payoff. Don't expect to continue your free-wheeling ways. The truth is that it's hard work. You have to sacrifice. You have to be upfront with friends and family. You have to tell your kids "no." But, remember the payoff. When the last card is off the list, you'll have $300 extra dollars a month to do whatever you want!

One thing . . . if you get into a bind and HAVE to pull out the card for an emergency, don't beat yourself up. Life happens. It's not the end of the world. Deal with it, and get back on track as soon as possible. Just push that spreadsheet out a few more months, and keep on whittling. Just like the dieter who eats the piece of birthday cake, it's a setback. Forget about the overindulgence, and get back to the work at hand.

Know Your Rights

Congress just passed a new credit card law designed to protect consumers from companies that have used tricks and traps to fool us. The law doesn't protect us from ourselves, though. It simply gives us the tools to make good decisions. It doesn't keep us from getting in over our heads.

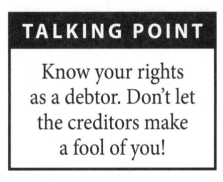

TALKING POINT

Know your rights as a debtor. Don't let the creditors make a fool of you!

Let's consider some provisions.

Credit card companies can't raise the interest rate they charge on existing balances. They can't change the rules in the middle of the game, so to speak. If you bought that pair of shoes when your rate was 10.5%, it should still be 10.5% when you pay them off. Remember, interest is the price of money, and an agreed upon price shouldn't be changed after purchase. However, there is an exception to this.

If you are 60 days late making a minimum payment on your

card, the company has the right to impose a penalty interest rate. I think that's fair enough. After all, if you're 60 days late on the payment, you're either a poor credit risk or very disorganized. Either way, it's your fault, and the credit company should be compensated. You've decided to treat your purchase of money as a layaway plan, so there should be additional charges. The lesson here is DON'T BE LATE!

Credit card companies are constantly changing their rates. The price of money varies, and credit card companies vary their price. They have the right to change their rates with each new purchase you make. The problem is that they were doing this so often, we found ourselves caught in a constantly escalating price environment. Now, they must send us a notice 45 days before the new rate takes affect. That gives customers enough time to shop around for a new, lower rate card.

Of course, this requires us to be proactive. If you get a notice of a rate increase, don't just sit there and take it. Go to sites like bankrate.com, creditcards.com, cardratings.com or cardtrek. com and find another option. If the guy cutting your grass told you he was raising his price by $25 a week, you'd start looking for another lawn man. Do the same with your credit card.

One trick Congress put a stop to was the short billing cycle. Those tricky credit guys liked to send bills that were due within a week of receipt. They counted on us delaying making a payment until the next time we pay bills. By that time, we found we were hit with a hefty late fee and additional interest charges . . . SOOO not fair! Now, they must mail statements at least 21 days before the due date. They didn't stop them from using odd due dates, though. My card is due on the 5th of the month, instead of the 1st or the 15th, which is when most other bills are due.

Pay close attention to your due date. If you pay your bills online like I do, make sure the payment gets there a day or two beforehand. Don't give them a reason to hit you with a fee. The new law says that as long as the payment is postmarked by 5 p.m. of the due date, it's on time. If the due date is on a Sunday or holiday, you have until the next day. This may be the only time I send a thank you note to my congressman!

Cards may also have different charges for different products. Cash advances may be at one interest rate, while purchases are at another rate. Before, companies could decide how they wanted to post payments. Of course, they tended to post the payment to the lowest rate balance! With the new law, they must post the payment to the highest rate item first.

Companies also love to tack on a lot of fees. Spending more than your allotted credit limit usually results in a fee. The new law says this is no longer an automatic fee.

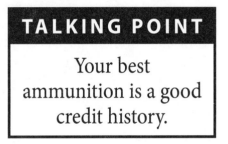

TALKING POINT

Your best ammunition is a good credit history.

The company must get your permission before they allow you to go over the limit and incur that fee. Now, that means you may, instead, incur some embarrassment when you have to put back a few items in order to get through the check out line. But embarrassment only costs you a little dignity. Always opt out.

One provision I'm particularly happy about has to do with minors. Congress says you must be an adult (21 years old) to have a credit card. Anyone under this age must have an adult as the primary accountholder. This should slow down the practice of going after college students. Card companies often purchase student lists from colleges and barrage freshmen with credit card offers. Colleges who allow this should be ashamed!

This will still allow parents peace of mind that their college students have access to credit to purchase necessary items, but it gives mom and dad the control over the amount and timing of purchases. For those 18 year olds who are on their own, you can still get a card, if you can show proof of income.

The credit card companies have been screaming about this new law. They have been trying to convince us that it will mean higher fees and rates. I say "hogwash." They may try to increase rates and institute new fees in the short-run, but in the long-run, competition will take over.

As a consumer, your best ammunition is a good credit history. This gives you the power to negotiate for the best rates and the lowest fees. Know that much of their profits come from the purchases at the cash register. They make from 1 to 2% of each total purchase from the retailer, so even if you pay off your bill each month, they want your business. Know your rights. Pay attention to your statements and to any correspondence from your company. Don't be afraid to speak up and ask for them to lower rates and waive fees. If they don't agree, go somewhere else. There are a million of these companies, and you only need ONE card! Shop around.[2]

---

2 Credit Card Act of 2009.

CHAPTER FOUR

Talking about Savings

Saving money is a good starting place for sound financial management. It depends on us having a little left over after paying the bills. That means we must be living within our means, if we want to have money TO save. As children, saving meant having a piggybank. There was something wonderful about dropping those coins in the slot on the top of the pig. We heard the clink of the coins and knew this money was safe from our easy grasp. When we got enough money to buy some treasured, anticipated item, we broke the bank.

Planning to Save

We first learn to save when we find ourselves short of the money needed to buy something we want. As a kid, that something could be a pair of roller skates or a video game. As an adult, that something could be a new sofa or the down payment on a house. Saving and anticipating got dealt a blow with the advent of easy credit. Why save for a new sofa when you can buy one now and not pay for it for twelve easy months?

The trap of easy credit is that, not only do we miss out on saving up for something, but we also stop saving for a rainy day. Life is full of uncertainties for families. The car breaks down. The roof starts leaking. You get laid off work. So, while saving for that something we want is the starting place, saving for the sake of saving is the goal. You do this by building in a savings amount into your monthly budget.

TALKING POINT

Use a bank draft to build savings. You'll never miss the money.

Maybe you start with only $10 or $20 a month, but you must start! Because when the uncertainties of life roll around (and they will), having a savings account to fall back on makes all the difference. It means you won't need to use a credit card to get you through the unexpected. You will have already planned for the unexpected with your rainy day fund.

Make this account separate from your household account. There should be a clear distinction, like the piggy bank. While you want the money to be accessible, you don't want it to be too easy to get your hands on it. You want to think twice before you break the bank.

Making Your Money Earn Money

Make sure this account earns a good interest rate. Don't expect your savings account to make what stocks and mutual funds make, but find a good short-term money market rate. Don't let your bank use your money for free. You can check your local banks to see what rates they are offering. Then, look online. Try bankrate.com to find savings rates from around the country.

Don't be afraid to open a bank account in another state. It's easy to do with a computer. Consider an online bank. Just make sure the bank is FDIC insured and has a good reputation. Beyond that, you're just looking for the most you can get for your money. Beware of limits on accounts. Some require minimum deposits. Some require monthly drafts. Make sure the one you choose fits your needs. Also, check with your employer. Many have existing credit unions that pay higher rates of interest than local banks. Using a credit union will also allow you to have your savings taken right out of your paycheck.

Consider setting up a bank draft for your savings account. You can set it up so that $50 goes into the account automatically. You'll be amazed how quickly this adds up. A bank draft imposes discipline—something most humans lack! If we have to DO something each time, it doesn't happen. Some will say, "Oh, I'll move over extra money every month," then never get around to it. If you set

TALKING POINT

Search online for the best savings rates. When it comes to savings, local may not be the best option.

up the draft, you have to DO something to stop it. The result is you do nothing, and your savings account grows!

Using Your Savings Account

Having a nice savings account takes the stress out of life. When the air conditioning breaks down, you don't panic. You know that you're covered. Pay cash for the new AC and go your merry way. Your budgeted savings will begin to replace what you took out and will be there the next time life hits you with another uncertainty.

For some, taking money out of a savings account is taboo. They are so afraid to break open the piggy bank that they pull out the credit card. Now, that doesn't make sense! Why would you pay 15% on a credit card while you have money in a savings account that is only earning 2%? Savings accounts are meant to be used. Note I didn't say they were meant to be sucked dry! Recognize that you are saving for emergencies. Give yourself permission to use the money when these emergencies occur.

Keeping More than One Account

I like things simple. That means I think you should have one household account and one savings account. Some folks like to have a savings account for everything under the sun. They'll have one account for their vacation, one for the new carpet, and one for the new refrigerator. That would drive me crazy! It also often dilutes your efforts, as you try to get the best rate on your savings.

Of course, with the ease of opening online accounts and the competition among banking institutions, it's not necessarily the case any longer. I guess I have to rethink this one. If having separate accounts helps you to keep it straight and it doesn't cost you in interest earnings, go for it. For me, it's better to keep

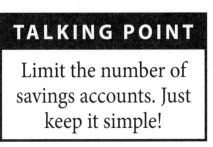

TALKING POINT

Limit the number of savings accounts. Just keep it simple!

one savings account. I know this money will accomplish many things for me, and I am clear on how much I need to keep for the emergencies. If you are tempted to use your rainy day fund for the trip to Hawaii instead of saving extra for that longed for trip, keep it in separate piggy banks. Basically, just do whatever works.

I'm a little morbid, though. I'm always thinking about what would happen if I got hit by a truck. Would my heirs be able to find all the accounts I opened? Would they know where everything is? What if I was in a coma and needed money to pay my bills? Could all my bits and pieces of savings be found? If you're going to complicate your life with multiple accounts, keep a good record of each AND talk to someone about that record.

How Much is Enough?

Of course, the question everyone asks is how much savings is enough. My answer? That depends.

Some advisors suggest three or six months of salary,[1] while

---

1 "The Emergency Fund" taken from Dave Ramsey, Suze Orman, and others.

others use some other formula. I think it depends on the security of your income. If you are a real estate agent or a car salesman, your earnings are in the form of commissions. When you make a sale, you make money. When you don't, you go hungry. Sales commission jobs offer very little security. When economic times are good, the pay is good, but when things go south, so does your paycheck.

If you are a self-employed person, your income fluctuates. Owning your own business leaves you completely vulnerable to the business cycle. When it's good, it's great, and when it's bad, it stinks. Any entrepreneur can tell you that if you want income security, don't start your own business.

And if you are employed by a company that is struggling, your income is uncertain. The tougher the times, the more likely you are to face a layoff or a reduction of working hours. So, when times start getting lean, that's when you need to get even more serious about building savings.

If you are a long-time government employee, you may not be concerned about fluctuating income. Or if you are retired and drawing a guaranteed pension, you may not be concerned about changes in income. Or if you have a trust fund paying you on a monthly basis, you may not be fazed by the business cycle. The more sure your income, the smaller the importance of a savings account.

Each family needs to sit down and decide on some savings goal. This is the number that will make you comfortable and allow you to sleep at night. You will know that whatever happens, you're covered. You won't need to whip out the credit card and call the bank for a loan. You've saved for the rainy day, the emergency.

Six months of income is a good rule of thumb in those uncertain income situations. If you're in the middle when it comes to uncertainty, three months may be plenty. Even if your income is guaranteed or very secure, though, you need to have something in savings. It's just a good practice.

TALKING POINT

How much savings you need depends on the security of your job.

I usually like to aim for a round number—maybe $3000 or $5000 or $10,000. How much you need depends on monthly expenses and lifestyle. Start saving and don't dip into this account until you reach your goal. After you hit the magic number, you can do two things. First, you can then use this money for bigger "wants." Also, you can use part of this money to invest in longer-term securities.

If your goal is $5000, always strive to keep at least this much in savings. If you take a trip and the account falls to $3500, work hard to get it back to your magic number. If you go through a period without a job and the account falls to $100, you'll need to make savings a priority as soon as you land another job. Once your family has its comfort number, develop a plan to get to that number and then maintain that amount.

Having a nice savings account doesn't take away the uncertainties in life. It just makes them more bearable.

CHAPTER FIVE

Talking about Mortgages

There are two parts to home ownership. One part is that a house is an investment. Like any investment, you don't want to lose money. At the very least, you want it to hold its value. More than likely, you expect to sell your house for more than what you paid.

The second part of home ownership is a bit fuzzier. Our house is our home. It's where we live and play and form family and community. Our house says something about us. It is a status symbol and a reflection of our personalities and values. Putting those two parts together is where we get into trouble.

The Investment Part

Real estate can be a good investment. Note I said "can." When you are ready to buy a house, you need to concentrate on the first part of home ownership by making sure your purchase is a good investment. Take care of part one first. Part two will follow.

Up until 2008 and the bursting of the real estate bubble, we expected real estate to only go up. Boy, was that a mistake! Real estate is an investment, and, like any investment with risks and rewards, it is just as likely to fall in value as it is to increase in value. Apparently, some folks forgot this rule of investing. They just observed everyone piling into real estate and jumped on the bandwagon. Approach home buying with caution.

Historically, real estate, on average, tends to gain 4-5% a year in value[1]. It tends to follow inflationary trends. While we all know the fish stories of the folks who bought a piece of land for $100,000 only to sell it six months later for $500,000, those stories are actually rare in real estate. Making money in real estate requires patience. This is a long-term investment.

TALKING POINT

The mantra of real estate is true—location, location, location!

The mantra of real estate REALLY is true—location, location, location. In particular, people are looking at the quality of life in a particular location. We all want the same things. We want good schools, safe streets, access to shopping, and strong communities. Most of us also prefer "new." We like new construction and new shopping areas and new streets with pretty

1 *Just Give Me the Answers* by Garrett and Swift.

landscaping. The exception to this may be in historic areas. There, we want the quaint old cottages, but we still prefer they have bright, shiny, new kitchens.

The problem with this mantra is that the hot location today may not be the hot location tomorrow. Populations shift. New developments are opened, and young families want to be in the center of the action. When choosing the best location for your money, make sure it is a location that is on the rise, not one on the downside.

Choosing a neighborhood is like choosing a stock sector in which to invest. If I believe the baby boom generation will be trying to stay young and vibrant, I might choose to invest in companies that make things like gym equipment or knee replacements or beauty cream or pharmaceuticals. When you are ready to choose a neighborhood, study the population in your area.

Where do people want to be? What neighborhoods are building houses that offer what folks are looking for? What amenities in the neighborhood do people find appealing? Does everyone in your area want to live in a townhouse with no upkeep, or do they want a three acre spread? At this point, forget about what YOU want. Just look at what everyone else is doing.

Once you have honed in on the best location(s), you must face the reality of your budget. List neighborhoods, in order of appeal. Then list the price ranges within each neighborhood. Some will be out of reach, so you'll just have to check them off the list. When you come up with a group with houses you can afford, then you're ready to start looking at individual houses.

Your goal is to buy the smallest house in the best neighborhood that you can afford. This will be your best investment, in that it offers you the best chance to make money. Of course, knowing this and following through on it are two very different things, since there is that other part of home ownership.

The Home Part

Our homes say something about us. They indicate our style, our status, and our values. So, when we step into the smallest home in the best location, we're often disappointed. We look at the neighbors across the street with their palatial digs, and we feel small. How can we possibly be happy in THIS home in THIS neighborhood? Real estate agents understand human behavior, and they know we don't always choose the best investment house. Emotions take over, and we end up spending more than we can afford and paying too much for that trophy house.

I'm not telling you to give up on the "home part." I'm recommending some sensible compromises. Style is one area of compromise. Choose a home that fits your way of living and your particular tastes. If you like front porches, look for a home in your location with that great porch. If you prefer columns and fancy front doors, look for that. Compromise on style by looking for style options in areas of the house — wood floor versus scored concrete, granite versus ceramic tile, porches versus decks. You may not get everything you want, but you may get some things that are true reflections of your personal style.

The catch on style is that you don't want to be too far out of the mainstream. If you buy a modern home in an area where everyone else likes traditional, you'll have trouble upon re-

a month on the principal and interest. Multiply that monthly amount by 360 payments (12 x 30 years), and you'll see that the total payout for your $150,000 mortgage is $323,757. If you choose a fifteen-year mortgage, the same $150,000 will cost you $1265 a month. While that's a big jump for a young family on a monthly basis, the total payout for this mortgage is only $227,841. That's about $100,000 less!

So, when you start out, you will probably take out a thirty-year mortgage, just because you can't afford the big monthly payment. As you build a little wealth and have better income, move to the fifteen-year option. You'll save yourself a ton of money!

Back to the sensibility of taking out a big loan to buy a house, mortgages are long-term debts, so their rates are typically lower than rates on things like cars and credit cards. Over the last few years, mortgage rates have been at historically low levels. As I write this, rates are in the 5-6% range.[3] I remember a time when mortgage rates were in the double-digit range! Talk about the high price of home ownership!

The lower the mortgage rate, the more house you can afford. Start by looking at how much you want to pay each month on a mortgage payment. Suppose that amount is $1000. If your mortgage rate is 5%, that translates to a $167,000 mortgage. If your mortgage rate is 8%, you can only afford a $136,000 mortgage. That's a big difference! It's one of the reasons the real estate market went crazy when mortgage rates began falling.

So, low interest rates make taking out a mortgage reasonable, but there is a bonus to this. Interest on mortgages is tax deductible. In fact, this is one of the few deductions left to us.

---

3 www.bankrate.com.

Let's go back to that $150,000 thirty-year mortgage. Your interest for the first full year of home ownership will be about $9000. If you earned $60,000, you will pay tax on only $51,000 after the deduction. Depending on your tax bracket, that deduction can save you anywhere from $1300 to $2500 (about). That tax savings reduces the actual cost of the loan. That 6% mortgage sounds great, but factor in the tax savings and it may only be costing you around 4.5 - 5%.

There are several mortgage calculators on the internet. Bankrate.com offers a good one. I'd recommend spending $30 and buying a financial calculator. In fact, some phones now offer a financial calculator. Learn how to do time value of money problems. It will be a tremendous help when you begin shopping for a home.

Remember, in normal times, real estate increases in value around 4% per year. We've all seen the craziness of 100% increases in a boom, but don't expect this to happen. Real estate (if you are wise on the location choice) will grow in value, but it grows slowly. A mortgage that only costs you about 4.5% coupled with a home that is increasing in value at a 4% rate is a good deal. If you're smart and don't take on TOO much house, you can end up coming out about even.

But who's happy with "even?"

Don't forget that you need a place to live. If you're not paying on your own home, you're paying for someone else's home in the form of rent. But rent, once it is paid, is gone for good. There is no return of your money when you leave the home. And you don't even get a tax break on the payments. While renting is a reasonable option for some families in some situations, the way to build wealth is to own your own house.

Each time you make a payment, it's like putting money into

an investment account. At the beginning of the mortgage, most of your payments go for interest. The longer you pay, the more of your payment goes towards the principal. Those monthly payments don't just provide you with a place to call your castle. They are part of your savings plan. As you pay back the mortgage company, you are paying yourself by building equity in the house. Equity is the word for the money that goes into your pocket when you sell your house. If you bought your home for $150,000, pay on it for five years, then find it is worth $183,000, you've made $33,000. Right? But if you sell the house in five years for $183,000, you'll end up with more than $33,000 in your pocket. That's because your mortgage balance has been declining with every payment you make.

That's the real beauty of home ownership. It gives us a place to call home, and it helps us to save at the same time. Now, instead of walking away with $33,000, we end up with about $43,000 in our pockets. We saved $10,000 without even thinking about it just by making our payments each month.

The Down Payment

Buying a house usually requires a down payment. The typical amount is 20% of the value of the home. For a $150,000 house, that means coming up with $30,000. Again, this seems out of reach for most young families. Lenders want us to have some of our own money in the deal. It gives them some assurance that we won't walk away from the house if times get tough.

While 20% should be your goal, you may not be able to do this until your second house. There are other options, but expect to pay something additional to give your lender some protection. This protection is called mortgage insurance. Typically, it is a premium that is added to your monthly payment. The amount you'll pay depends on the price of the house. On a $150,000

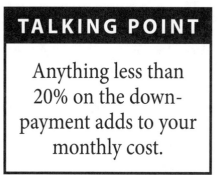

TALKING POINT

Anything less than 20% on the down-payment adds to your monthly cost.

mortgage, your PMI (stands for Private Mortgage Insurance) will run you about $150 per month.[4]

This is not a little number. On our original calculation for a $150,000 mortgage at 6%, this represents more than a 15% increase in your monthly payment. Your $899 payment just turned into about $1050 a month. It could be the difference in steak or macaroni and cheese for supper every night! Make sure you know this number going into the deal. It's part of the cost of home ownership for anyone putting less than 20% down.

If you are a veteran or are currently in the military, you may qualify for a VA mortgage with NO down payment.[5] That's right. There is an option for a mortgage through this government entity that doesn't require a penny up front. (It's another reason to serve your country!) Of course, they will usually require some sort of insurance. In this case, though, that may be just one year's worth of mortgage insurance or about $1800 for the $150,000 loan.

In lower priced markets, down payments (non-VA) don't

4 "Understanding the Cost of Private Mortgage Insurance," Univ. of West Georgia.
5 "What is a VA Loan?," www.valoans.com.

usually dip below 10%. So, even on that $150,000, you'll need $15,000 just to get into the house. Then, you'll be facing an extra $150 per month for mortgage insurance. In higher priced markets, down payments may only be 5%. Federal bond money sometimes becomes available, and these loans only require 3% down. For the federal money, you'll need to fit the qualifiers. Talk to your real estate agent.

While paying mortgage insurance each month is not the ideal, it is one way to get started on accumulating wealth in real estate without waiting until you've saved enough pennies. Be aware that this insurance is not meant to last forever. If your house gains in value and you have paid down enough on the loan, you may be able to ask for this insurance to be dropped. That's right. You can request a new appraisal and a review on this requirement.

This is how it works. Suppose you've lived in the house about five years, faithfully making your payments on the $150,000 mortgage. You now only owe about $140,000. You notice that houses in your neighborhood are selling for $175,000 to $200,000. If your home appraises for at least $175,000, you can get relief. Do the math. Take $140,000 and divide it by 0.80 (or 1 minus the 20% down payment requirement). If the appraisal comes in higher than $175,000, your payment drops about $150 a month. Talk about a savings.

The lesson here is that if you have to take out mortgage insurance, pay attention to the current value of your home and the amount you owe on the mortgage. You will probably have to pop for the appraisal, but it will be worth it. Just don't pull the trigger on this too soon and waste the time and money. But when the time is right, this is a bonanza for your family.

Escrow

Most lenders want to make sure that you are paying your property taxes and your property insurance. After all, they don't want to be left holding the bag if someone buys the house in a tax sale or if the house burns down without insurance. They are just protecting their interests.

They do this be requiring an escrow account. That just means that the lender/mortgage company will pay the taxes and property insurance each year. Of course, they don't do this for free. They collect extra each month from you to cover these bills when they come due. If your property insurance is $400 a year and your property tax is $1200 per year, they will add about $135 a month to your payment. Multiply $135 by 12 months, and you'll get a little over $1600.

If you have a fixed mortgage at 6%, your payment to the mortgage company for the $150,000 loan will stay at $899 for the life of the loan—all 30 years. But your monthly payment may change from year to year because of the escrow account. When you first buy the house, the mortgage company will calculate the "extra" amount by looking at property taxes and insurance from the previous year. But these amounts can change.

Property taxes may go up. The county tax assessor may suddenly decide your house is worth more than is now on the books, or the tax rate may be raised. Property insurance changes from year to year. Just ask those folks within the scope of Hurricane Katrina. They suddenly found themselves with property insurance increases in the thousands! Suddenly, your payment to the mortgage company may look minor compared to the insurance.

We have a beach house, and we faced such increases. Some of our neighbors told about insurance premiums jumping to

$30,000 per year! Remember, if you have a mortgage on the property, the lender will force you to buy protection. When this happens, you have three choices. You can pay off the mortgage (and few can do that). You can pay the huge payment each month. Or you can let the property go back to the bank, and many people have done just that.

Property taxes and insurance are part of the cost of home ownership. Find out what these exact costs will be. Call your insurance agent and get a quote. Ask about any unusual situations (like hurricanes or earthquakes) in the area that may affect this in the future. Call the county clerk's office and get the latest property tax.

One caution, if you are buying a new house, you may get a surprise after the first of the year. If the last time the property was appraised, there was no house on it, it's still being taxed like an empty lot. The mortgage company only escrows taxes based on the previous year, so they will get a notice saying your escrow account is short.

Suppose the taxes went from $400 for an empty lot to $1200 for a new home. The lender is short $800. Before, they were escrowing about $66 ($400 for property insurance plus $400 for property tax) a month to cover the extras. Now, they must collect the shortage of $800, AND they must prepare for a higher bill next year of $1200. That means your payment for extras just went from $66 a month to $200 a month! (That's $800 shortage plus $1200 for next year's taxes plus $400 for insurance.)

Each year, you will get a statement from your mortgage company explaining this escrow account. Again, if you have a fixed rate mortgage, it's not the payment to the lender that changes. It's those extras. Be aware of the pitfalls.

Arms and Legs in Mortgages

There are different types of mortgages. The plain vanilla type is called a fixed mortgage. That means the interest rate you are being charged is "fixed" or the same for the life of the loan. If you take out a fixed rate mortgage at 6%, it will be 6% if you pay off the loan in thirty years. Fixed rate mortgages don't change their rates. If your rates don't change, your payments don't change.

I like fixed rate mortgages because you know, for certain, what that basic payment will be the whole time you own the house. There are no surprises. The last several years, we have seen historically low interest rates on mortgages. I've been saying FOR SEVERAL YEARS, if you can't afford a fixed rate thirty-year mortgage on the house, you can't afford the house! Walk away and don't let some real estate agent or some mortgage broker convince you otherwise.

You don't have to be a finance professor to know when rates are low. Most people have some knowledge about interest rates. If you're clueless, though, do some research to get an historical perspective. For goodness sake, GOOGLE it! If rates are low, and you think they may go up in the next five years, your best bet is to lock in the low fixed rate now. It's a no brainer. You don't even need to look at another option.

ARMs, in mortgages, are adjustable rate mortgages. Adjustable means they don't stay the same.

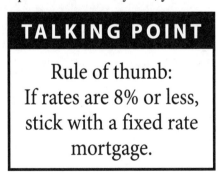

TALKING POINT

Rule of thumb:
If rates are 8% or less,
stick with a fixed rate
mortgage.

Your basic payment will "adjust" depending on the movement of interest rates. ARMs are good if interest rates are on the high side and you expect them to go lower. In that case, you want to take advantage of lower rates in the future. The biggest problem with ARMs is their uncertainty. For a young family, an adjustment in the wrong direction can be devastating. You could see your basic payment change by $200 or more.

The reason ARMs are popular is that they tend to offer lower rates than fixed mortgages. Lenders WANT to be able to adjust their loans to changing interest rates. They don't want to be stuck with a 6% loan when new loans are charging 8%. In order to get you to bite on their ARM, they must offer you something in exchange. That something is usually a lower upfront rate than a fixed mortgage.

There are all kinds of variations on ARMs. Some are fixed for as long as five years. Most are fixed annually. That means you get a new calculated payment on the anniversary of the loan. Some are adjusted every two years. Most have a lot of legal and financial jargon explaining how the calculation is done. It makes ME roll my eyes back in my head. All of it is designed to benefit the lender. Trust me. They're not thinking about you!

Home buyers are enticed by ARMs because it lets them buy more house than they can really afford. The payments begin to climb after the first year or so, and before you know it, you're in over your head. It's a dangerous game to play, even for the most astute financier.

There are other, even more dangerous, loans out there. Some are IOs. That stands for interest only, and it's very bad news! It means you will never build equity in the house, which is how you accumulate wealth. All you are doing is paying interest on the loan. NEVER, EVER do this type of loan. Another type allows you to adjust your payment based on various options. They usually set three or four payment plans. One usually includes an IO option. Stay away from these, as well. Many of these weird mortgages penalize you when you try to get out of them. A good rule of thumb is to stick with a fixed rate mortgage for rates at 8% or less. Even above 8%, be careful. Don't let your mortgage payment become a moving target in uncertain times.

Refinancing

Choosing a fixed rate mortgage doesn't commit you to that loan as long as you own the house. You always have the option to pay off the current loan, replacing it with a lower interest rate loan. I've played this game many times, but you have to be careful with the costs you incur each time you refinance.

The cost to refinance is usually around 1% to 1.5% of the loan.[6] This will vary with lenders. Be sure to get this spelled out before you begin. The rule of thumb often quoted is that you should refinance if the current rate is 2% lower than your existing mortgage.

I suggest looking at absolute dollar numbers. If your $150,000 loan is at 8%, your basic payment (without escrow) is around $1100. If the current mortgage rate is 6%, your payment will drop about $200 a month. If the closing costs run around $1500, it will take you eight months to make up those costs by your monthly savings. Run the numbers to see how long it will take you to cover the costs of the new loan.

---

6 *A Consumer's Guide to Mortgage Refinancing*, Federal Reserve Board.

Try one of the online calculators or use a financial calculator. Most mortgage brokers will also run this for you. You may find that a 1% interest rate difference is worth it for you. You must consider the actual dollar figures on your loan. What will be the monthly savings versus the cost to refinance? Then, you must determine if you will stay in the house long enough to recoup the cost. Remember, the costs of the refinance will be added to what you already owe. You won't have to pay these up front. They will become part of your loan.

TALKING POINT

Calculate the months it will take to make up the cost to refinance. You may find you don't have the time.

Again, the rule of thumb is a two year window. Again, I'll say that you need to run the numbers for your particular situation. If you plan on moving within the year, the chances are pretty good that you don't need to refinance. Regardless, get out the calculator and a pencil and paper before you jump into a refinance.

APR

When you start to shop for a loan, whether it's for a new purchase or for a refinance, you'll be hit with two numbers. The first one will be in BIG, BOLD print. It will be the stated interest rate. Ignore this number.

For the borrower, the only number that counts is the APR.

This is the annual percentage rate. It takes into account all the closing costs that will be added to your loan. When you take out a $150,000 loan, you don't repay just $150,000. You repay $150,000 plus whatever they charge for doing the loan. That means you'll pay back from $151,500

TALKING POINT

Forget those rates listed in BIG numbers. Find "APR" on the statement to find out what you're REALLY paying.

to $152,250 (about). If the mortgage broker quotes you a stated rate of 6%, and the closing costs are $2250, your APR is 6.15%.

Insist on seeing a detailed listing of closing costs. They will be able to give you a good faith estimate. Find the APR. You may have to get out your magnifying glass, but this is the only number that counts. It allows you to compare mortgages.

Remember, APR. Ask for it from the mortgage broker. Use it to compare lenders.

Other Costs

A final word on home ownership . . .

In addition to the mortgage, the insurance, and the property tax, there are other costs to home ownership. When you are a tenant and the air conditioner breaks down, you call the landlord. When you own the house, you have to pay the bill yourself to replace the AC.

Your house is an investment, and it's important to keep it in tip-top shape. Regularly walk around your property and look for potential problems. Consider regular maintenance costs like painting and cleaning. Heating and AC units don't last forever. Roofs have to be replaced. Wood rots. Build a maintenance account into your monthly budget to cover these costs.

As you look at potential homes, consider future costs of maintaining the home. The older the home, the higher the maintenance costs. Ask to see the disclosure statement listing the ages of the appliances, the heating and AC, and the roof. An inspection on older homes is important. The inspector can point out potential problems. Know what you're getting into before you make the offer.

On a new home, you'll have the benefit of lower maintenance costs, but you may face higher expenses on landscaping. Don't forget the yard when calculating maintenance costs. Also, with a new home, you'll probably have to pay for window treatments, while older homes generally come with these.

Finally, consider utility costs. Older homes with less insulation will cost more to heat and cool. Larger homes suck up more energy. Expect a big water bill on a house with a pool.

And don't forget homeowner's associations. Some neighborhoods don't have these, so there is no fee. We have a small association, so our cost is about $200 a year. For a townhouse or apartment, fees could be $200 a month or more. Consider these monthly fees as part of owning the home. If you don't pay them, the association can take out a lien against the house and collect the fees upon sale. Fees are related to the amenities of the neighborhood. Clubhouses, pools, gyms, gates, landscaping, etc. add to the value of the neighborhood. Expect to pay for them.

Don't let all these costs scare you away. Remember, home

ownership is a great way to accumulate wealth while you create a home for your family. Treat your house as an investment first. The "home" part will naturally follow.

CHAPTER SIX

Talking about Other Debt

Debt seems to be the American way. In China, the average savings rate is around 25%.[1] Before the financial meltdown, our average savings rate was 0%. Now that we're all running scared, that has jumped to 5.7%. That's a good thing!

Some financial advisors preach on the evils of debt. They propose living on a cash basis. I'm not one of those. I simply don't think that's reasonable for most families. Who can actually do that?

I think using debt to buy a house is wise. It allows you to have a home and build wealth at the same time. On the other hand, I sing to the heavens about the evils of credit card use.

---

1 "China's Consumers: Too Scared to Spend," *BusinessWeek;* "Get Out the Wallets," *Newsweek.*

The interest rates are high, and the stuff you're buying isn't going to improve your balance sheet. In fact, most of it will be long gone before you make that final payment.

Car Loans

There are some in-between areas where debt may make sense. Some people live in urban areas and can use public transportation. For most of us, we need a car to get back and forth to work. Few people can pay cash for a car. In this case, taking on debt allows us to generate more income.

Of course, many people view their cars the same way that they view their houses. They are status symbols. They say something about our personality and our values. Personally, I want to look cute, yet refined in my vehicle. Some guys need a BIG truck that makes a lot of noise going down the highway. Some women need the Volkswagon with the flower in the dash. Some people want to show that they are concerned about the environment by driving around in their Prius.

Cars and trucks are transportation. Their only real value lies in their ability to help us produce an income. With a house, you have an investment. With a vehicle, you have an immediate loss as soon as you drive it off the lot because of depreciation. Your car will never be worth more than on the day you make the purchase. While I could tell you to go out and buy a clunker to drive to work, I know you won't do it. So, I'm not even going to waste my breath.

Instead, I'm going to tell you to be reasonable. Look at your other monthly expenses and figure out how much you can afford each month in a car payment. Do this BEFORE you step on the lot. Base your calculation on 48 easy months. Don't get suckered into 60 or 72. Use a financial calculator or find one on the internet.

Dealers often offer special interest rates, but there is a catch. You have to have good credit to qualify. Before you are enticed by the 0% ad, get them to run your report to see if you can get the deal. Don't get behind the wheel of ANY car until you know you can afford it. Car salesmen know they can get you by getting you to take the drive first. You fall in love with the car, and bam! Before you know it, you own a car you can't afford.

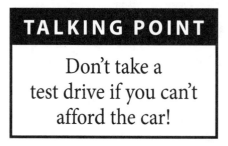

TALKING POINT

Don't take a test drive if you can't afford the car!

Consider a used car. They've already depreciated in value and may be a better deal. But be cautious. Get any used car checked out by a reliable mechanic. Also, loans on used cars are usually of a shorter term than those for new cars. That means you may face a higher payment on that used car.

Remember, there are other costs associated with owning a car. You'll need insurance. This varies, depending on the car and driver. New, expensive cars have higher premiums than old clunkers. Check with your insurance agent before you go shopping. Also, you'll need a license. The higher the price tag on the car, generally, the higher the car tag. Call your county clerk to find out the license fee. If you live in an urban area, you may also face monthly parking fees.

Before you step on the car lot, do the math. Calculate monthly payments, based on your credit. Find out insurance costs and tag fees. Consider any other additional costs like parking fees.

And don't forget maintenance and fuel. You'll have to get the oil changed occasionally. The tires will have to be replaced eventually. You'll have to gas up that big truck every week. Add it all up.

Once you've done this, you can go shopping. Now, you can get the cute or the BIG or the "green" as long as it's in your budget!

Educational Debt

There is another type of debt that makes sense because it is an investment in future income. It's educational debt. Taking out loans to further your education may mean an increase in income. Of course, make sure that the amount of future income is enough to pay back that debt.

Don't take out $100,000 in loans to become a social worker. The pay for social workers is not high and doesn't warrant that kind of debt. Before you pursue the degree, check out the job market and incomes for the degree. Look at job sites and find out average annual incomes for the types of jobs you'll qualify for after completing the education.

Think of the DIFFERENCE in income and how you can use that to pay back the loan. If you're making $40,000 a year now but expect a $10,000 increase with a new degree, it will take 5 years to pay back $50,000 in school loans. After 5 years, you will earn that extra money until retirement debt-free.

This also means that you should make sure you can work long enough to pay off the loans and end up with extra money in your pocket. Pursuing a law degree at age 50 may be a stretch but going for it at age 30 may make perfect sense. In some cas-

> **TALKING POINT**
>
> # Don't take out school loans for a job paying minimum wage!

es, you may need to quit your current job in order to go to school. Don't forget to factor in the lost income from those years.

A degree is an investment. You must ask the question, "What will this be worth in the job market?" Then consider all the costs of pursuing the education. When all is said and done, will you be ahead?

Types of Educational Loans

There are 2 types of educational loans: subsidized and unsubsidized. Anyone can qualify for unsubsidized loans. The "un" part means that the federal government is not offering any assistance on these loans. Interest accumulates while you are going to school. Subsidized loans are granted based on income and assets. Generally, the interest clock doesn't start ticking until you finish the degree. With any educational loan, you will have to complete a form called FAFSA.[2] Every college/university has an office that can help you navigate these waters.

Interest rates on educational loans are usually lower than, say, a car loan, but higher than a mortgage rate. Typically, they are a pretty good deal. Payments kick in six months after graduation, and you can choose a payment plan based on a number of years. Try to clear these out as soon as possible. Aim for five years. You don't want to be paying on your student loans at the

---

2 www.fafsa.ed.gov.

same time that you are sending your teenager to college!

Interest on educational loans may also be tax deductible. Talk to your CPA. The deduction lowers the actual cost of the debt, making these loans appealing.

One more thing... if you get into a bind, you can ask for a forbearance. That means you can stop paying on the loans for a period of time. Of course, the interest is still accumulating, so only do this as a last resort. Currently, students who graduate with loans have an average of $22,000 in debt. Remember, taking on debt to further your education only makes sense if the increase in income is enough to cover the debt payments and still leave you with money in your pocket.

And when you start having children, think about how it felt to pay off those loans. The greatest gift you can give your children is a debt-free degree, but to do that you have to start planning and saving as soon as they're born!

CHAPTER SEVEN

Talking about Saving for College

A college education is a must in our society, but the expense keeps getting higher. Parents should start planning for college as soon as they get home from the hospital.

I'm not kidding!

Have you checked out the cost of a college degree?

The average annual cost for a four year public university is now around $18,000.[1] In 18 years, you can expect that cost to be between $30,000 and $35,000. Multiply that by four, and you get into six figures. Add in a year for goofing off, and the tab keeps rising. Tack on graduate school, and you can start to feel weak. What if you want to send Junior to Harvard? Better

---

1 "2008-09 College Prices," www.collegeboard.com.

prepare for around half a million dollars for when the toddler turns into a college freshman.

College is an expensive proposition. Not only do you face tuition and books, but there are living expenses. When you send your children off to college, you are actually supporting two households. Most parents face this at the same time that they are staring their own retirement in the eyes. It's crazy to wait until high school to start thinking about how to pay for this venture.

While your genius may end up with a full scholarship, I think it's best to prepare for the worst and hope for the best. Enlist the help of family members. I find that many grandparents want to set up educational plans for the kiddies. It's a wonderful, long-lasting gift. When all is said and done, you will probably use savings, student loans, work programs, and scholarships. But, for now, let's talk about saving for college.

Prepaid Tuition

Most states offer two types of college savings programs. One is a form of prepaid tuition, and it works like insurance. You decide on the coverage you need. Then, you pay the premiums based on that coverage.

Mississippi's prepaid program is called MPACT.[2] I'll concentrate on this one, but other states have similar models. You are locking in the current cost of tuition for your child. With educational costs rising higher than inflation, this is a good deal. And it is guaranteed. There is no risk of losing money in the stock market with this type of plan.

---

2 www.collegesavingsmississippi.com.

Mississippi offers flexibility in its options. You can buy one year of coverage at a four year university or one year at a community college. You can add on years, up to five, in any combination of university and community college. The price is based on the current age of your child.

You may choose to pay the premium in a lump sum or pay it in monthly increments. One mom told me about writing her check each month to MPACT. She would always tell her son that she was paying for his college with each monthly payment. One day, the six year old said, "Do I have to go now?" I think telling your children about saving for college encourages them to prepare for the event, as well.

Mississippi was late to the game in offering these plans. My daughter was 16 years old when MPACT first became available. I purchased a plan for her in a lump sum. It cost a little over $10,000, and I was able to deduct this from my state income tax (a nice savings). She graduated in 1999, as the stock market was peaking. As she

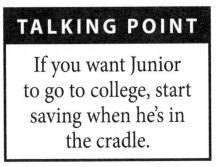

TALKING POINT

If you want Junior to go to college, start saving when he's in the cradle.

headed to college, stocks were dropping double digits while college tuition was increasing by like amounts. It was one of my best investments.

There is one bit of confusion about these plans. Parents think their kids have to go to an in-state school to use the plan. That is not the case. My daughter went to an out-of-state private school the first year, then came back to Mississippi to a private institution for the remainder of her education. MPACT paid the weighted average of the in-state public universities to the private institutions. All she had to do was flash the MPACT card. The school billing office took care of the rest. Of course, the private school was more expensive, so I had to pay the difference.

Mississippi's plan is run by the State Treasurer's office. You can find information on these plans online at www.collegesavingsmississippi.com. You must be a resident of Mississippi OR the child must be a resident of Mississippi to open an account. It doesn't have to be both. If you live in another state, check with your Treasurer's office about prepaid options. Most states have college savings plans. Earnings from these plans are exempt from taxes.

What if Junior runs off and joins the commune? Most states allow you to transfer accounts to other family members. If your genius gets the full scholarship OR bails on college all together, and you don't have anyone to transfer the account to, you can get back your money plus interest.

While MPACT is great, it only covers tuition and fees. Any parent can tell you that living expenses will be as much or more than the tuition. Locking in tuition is great, but it's only one piece of the puzzle.

529 Plans

States also offer another type of college savings plan. This is called a 529 plan.[3] The money in these plans can be used for any type of educational expense. They are not limited to tuition and fees. You can use them to pay for living expenses. You can

---

3 IRS Publication 970.

even use them for graduate school. As such, they offer more flexibility than the prepaid plans.

One difference, though, they are NOT guaranteed. 529 plans are investment accounts. Like any investment account, they are only as good as the investments. If you have a stock fund in your 529 and the market goes south, the account goes south. If you have a money market in your 529 plan, you'll only earn a small amount of interest, but you won't risk the funds.

While prepaid plans are like insurance, 529s are like 401(k)s. Once you open the account, you decide how much to put in. You decide on the funds to invest in. When Junior heads to college, whatever the value of the account is, that's what you can spend. You have to do your homework in selecting the best investment option for your child. If you're clueless, you may try choosing the option that is geared to your child's age. It works like those life cycle funds in retirement accounts—more aggressive when they are young, and getting safer the closer they get to college.

Remember, 529 plans are set up by each state. In Mississippi, the plan is called MPACT and is administered by TIAA-CREF.[4] Each state selects its administrator and the set of funds that are offered within the plan. You don't have to live in Mississippi to open a Mississippi 529. Mississippians can open a 529 for Rhode Island's plan. You can choose any state in the union, but DON'T!

As a Mississippian, if I open an MPACT account for my child, I get a tax break on my state income tax for the amount I put in. If I open an account in Rhode Island, I DON'T! So, if your state offers decent options, you are better off using their 529 and getting the tax break. Any broker who tries to convince

---

4 www.collegesavingsmississippi.com.

you to hop to another state is only trying to generate higher commissions!

The money in 529 plans must also be used for educational purposes. The account can also be transferred to another family member, just like the prepaid plan. With prepaid tuition and 529 plans, the expenses are for HIGHER education, meaning they are designed for college students.

Check out the options in your state. Most offer both, a prepaid tuition program and a 529 plan. This is the starting place for your college savings plan for your child. Start with a prepaid plan, and then consider adding a 529 account, if you have the funds. Find information on your state's offering on the web. Most sites plainly list the options and explain how the accounts work. If you're still confused, pick up the phone and call the Treasurer's office.

Coverdell Education Savings Account

The Coverdell[5] account is part of federal law. These accounts must be used for educational purposes, but there is one key difference. They are not limited to college education expenses. You may use these for private school on the primary or secondary level.

There is an annual contribution limit of $2000,[6] and you receive no tax deduction on either the federal or state level. They work like a Roth IRA—no tax break upfront, but tax-free on the distributions as long as they are for educational purposes. You can open an account at a bank, mutual fund, or brokerage

---

5 IRS Publication 970.

6 www.savingforcollege.com.

house. Like a 529 plan, this is an investment account and is subject to the risks of the investments you choose.

Also, like a Roth IRA, there are income limits. You can only contribute if your income is below the federal limit. Currently, this is around $100,000 for a single person and $200,000 for a married couple. Look on irs.gov for information on income limits.

These accounts are ideal for parents who anticipate using private school for their children. Of course, the small annual contribution of $2000 won't take you far! And the income limits cut into their use. For these reasons, Coverdell accounts are few and far between.

IRA Account

If you're faced with saving for college AND saving for retirement, there's another option. You can take penalty-free withdrawals from IRA accounts, IF you use them for educational purposes.[7] For parents faced with both tasks, this may be the best option.

Sock away as much as possible in your Roth IRA. If Junior goes to college, you can use your own retirement account to offset college expenses. If he heads to the commune, the money is still yours. Another advantage of this approach is that a parent's retirement accounts may not count as much against the child when trying to qualify for aid.

So, there you have it. Start with state plans. Ask family members to use these accounts for birthday, Christmas, and graduation gifts. Use a Coverdell if you're facing private school on

---

7 IRS Publication 590.

the lower level. Fund your own Roth IRA, and prepare to use it for education. Look for scholarships. Apply for financial aid. Get Junior a job. Then, maybe, just maybe, you'll have enough to put him through college.

And, for goodness sake, prepare him to take care of you in your old age! After you get through educating him, there may be nothing left!

CHAPTER EIGHT

Talking about Retirement

It's Never Too Early to Start

Retirement always seemed so far away. When I was 16 and just getting started in my working life, I couldn't imagine retirement. After all, I was never going to get old. Then when I finished college and headed into my real career, I was only interested in making my mark in the world. In my mid-40s retirement started taking on real meaning. About that time, I realized that I was closer to retirement than to the start of my career. I was beginning the "wind down" time, and I needed to be ready for the day when I would no longer earn money.

Mostly, I work with retired clients. Their work is finished. They have earned every penny they will ever earn. Their only income comes from Social Security and investment earnings. And what I hear and sense from them is fear because no matter how much they've put aside, they are always afraid that it won't be enough. Retirement sounds all rosy, but the knowledge that you CAN'T get another job is another thing all together. The fear comes with the uncertainty of the end of life. How long will you live? Will you be able to take care of yourself, or will you need help in old age? What kind of health issues will you face? These are scary questions with no sure answers.

For that reason, I tell everyone to start saving early for retirement. In fact, I encourage parents to open IRA accounts for their children as soon as those teenagers start getting paychecks. A teenager who begins a retirement account certainly knows the wonder of compound interest. It can put you decades ahead in preparing for retirement. Waiting until retirement feels "real" before you start saving puts you behind the eight ball.

We know that we live, on average, 20 years after we retire.[1] Of course, we all know of family members who live much longer than that. In the United States, we are seeing rapid increases in the numbers of centenarians. Because we do not know how many years to prepare for, we need to start saving early and save a lot to get ready for the fallow time of our lives.

Remember the magic of compound interest. This allows our money to continue working for us, even if we aren't adding to the pot. So, as soon as you or your child get that first job, start saving for retirement. When looking for the first job out of college, ask about the company retirement plan. Each time you change jobs, sign up for the new retirement plan and make

---

1 "Senior Series: Facts About Retirement," The Ohio State University Extension.

decisions about the old plan. Whether you're 16 or 60, retirement savings should be a priority.

Suppose you have saved $5000 in a retirement account by the time you are 20 years old. If that account earns an average 7% each year, and you don't put another dime into it, you'll have $105,000 at age 65. If you wait until you're 45 to start saving for retirement, you'll have to put aside more than $2500 EACH year for 20 years to get that same $105,000 at age 65. Youth really is wasted on the young!

TALKING POINT

Open a Roth IRA for your teenager with his summer income.

One word of caution, though, retirement accounts are linked to earnings. You can't have a retirement account unless you have earned income. Earned income means you are getting a paycheck. If you get a W-2, you have earned income. If you pay self-employment tax, you have earned income. Earned income does NOT come from interest on CDs or other investments. Income from babysitting jobs that is not reported to the IRS is not earned income, as far as Uncle Sam is concerned.

Employer Retirement Plans

Typically, the best place to save for retirement is through an employer plan. There are two types of employer plans. One is called a Defined Benefit Plan. With this, our retirement is defined by our benefits package — our annual salary. These are often called pension plans.

With a pension plan, you have little to no risk. Your employer sets aside a certain amount of money for you. Your employer monitors the investments in the plan and bears the risks of those investments. You don't have to decide how much to set aside with each paycheck. You don't have to choose investments. All you have to do is keep showing up for work. A calculation using your salary determines how much money you will get each month in retirement.

Sounds great, huh?

Well, the problem is that these plans are going the way of the dinosaur. General Motors set up the first defined benefit plan in 1950.[2] The burden for retirees contributed to their demise in 2009. Employers no longer want to bear the risk for our retirement. Old-line companies with pension plans are freezing those plans while newer companies are not even offering this option.

Companies that still have pension plans pay into an insurance program to protect retirees against bankruptcy. The Pension Benefit Guaranty Corporation steps in to make monthly payments when companies disappear or reorganize, but the system has been overwhelmed because of tough economic times.

Because of these changes, most younger workers will never see such a plan. Instead, we are dependent on the second type of retirement plan—the Defined Contribution Plan.[3] They are called a variety of names such as 401(k), 403b, Deferred Compensation, etc. With this, our retirement is defined by our contributions. As employees, we bear ALL the risk for our retirement. We decide how much to take out of our paycheck. We decide which investments to use. If we don't put any money in,

---

2 "Defined Benefit and Defined Contribution Plans: A History, Market Overview and Comparative Analysis" by McCourt.
3 *ibid.*

TALKING POINT

At the VERY least, contribute the amount of the match.

we have nothing at retirement. If we choose bad investments, we're sunk.

With the decline in Social Security and the rise in defined contribution plans, the need for financial education has increased. You see, it doesn't matter whether you are a Wall Street investment banker or a plumber. Your retirement depends on how well you can understand the world of finance. And don't let anyone fool you into thinking a mere plumber can't save and invest. Hogwash! Everyone HAS to save for retirement. Everyone CAN get educated about retirement and investment options. We must! And we must do it like our lives depend on it, because they do!

Choosing a Contribution Rate

Most of the time when I ask someone how much they are contributing to their retirement plan, they can't tell me. They chose some rate 10 years ago, when they started the job. They haven't looked at it since. We usually have to look at their pay stub to figure it out. This should be like your mortgage interest or the interest on your credit card. You should know this number off the top of your head!

Sometimes, when I ask about a contribution rate, I get a smug look and the person will say, "I'm doing the maximum." I ask, "And what is that rate?" Their reply? "I don't know. I just know it's the maximum." Upon further probing, I find that their definition of "maximum" is related to the company match, not IRS limits.

Companies may OR may not offer a matching contribution. They are not required to match your contributions, but they may decide to make this a part of their plan as a way to encourage participation. Even companies who have a match may choose to forego the match during difficult economic times. In 2009, several companies have done just that.[4]

I've actually had folks tell me they wouldn't contribute because there was no match. Now, that's just cutting off your nose to spite your face! Remember, it's your retirement. If you don't save, you don't have any money. While a company match is nice, it shouldn't prevent you from contributing.

If there IS a company match, you want to take advantage of it. Suppose your company will match your contributions dollar for dollar up to 5%. Putting 5% in your retirement account means you immediately double your money! You put in 5%, and your company puts in 5%. What a deal! You can't find returns like that anywhere.

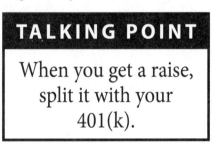

TALKING POINT

When you get a raise, split it with your 401(k).

Some matches are fifty cents for every dollar, or they offer some combination match. Ask the personnel department or read the plan. As an employee, you should receive something called a Summary Plan Description. This describes how your employer's retirement plan works. If it looks like Greek to you, ask for help in deciphering the legal jargon. Find out how the match works.

---

4 "Companies rethink 401(k) matches," *USA Today.*

ALWAYS, AT LEAST, take advantage of the matching money. Not participating in a plan when there is matching money is like walking past a five dollar bill without bothering to bend down and pick it up. That would be crazy, right? Free money is free money. In this case, it requires a little something from you, but the effort is minimal.

So, your starting point for a contribution rate is the match point. In fact, those folks who tell me they are contributing the maximum are usually referring to the match. They think they are tapped out at the point. No way! Only contributing to the match won't get you where you need to go.

Find out what the maximum percentage is for your plan. This will be based on your income and on current IRS regulations. In 2009, 401(k) contributions have a maximum allowable contribution of $16,500.[5] This amount is adjusted each year. If you are over 50 years old, there will be a catch-up contribution. Currently, that is $5,500, for a total of $22,000.[6]

Few people ever reach the maximum. We want to retire well-off, but we also have to pay the bills in the meantime. Know the maximum, and make it your ultimate goal. A good rule of thumb on the way to the ultimate goal is a contribution rate of 10%. You can fool yourself into increasing that amount by gradually adding 1% each year or each quarter. Remember this money is not taxed for income tax purposes, so the dollar that goes into your retirement account only feels about like seventy-five cents less in your paycheck. You will hardly notice the change, but it will make a huge difference over the years.

Also, if you get a raise, split the difference between your

---

5 IRS Publication 575.

6 IRS Publication 575.

pocket and your retirement account. If your raise is 4%, immediately increase your retirement contribution 2%. Do this before the raise kicks in, and you really won't miss it. You'll have more money in your pocket, and you'll be kicking your retirement savings into high gear.

Choosing Investments for Your Plan

With a 401(k) or any other defined contribution plan, you have to choose a set of investments. This is where most people's eyes roll back in their heads! Okay, so MAYBE you can choose how much to put in the plan, but how are you supposed to know how to invest those contributions? It seems that every average Joe has to be a financial whiz to figure this out. I'm here to tell you, "No, you don't!"

Every employer retirement plan has a plan menu. Choosing a combination of investments is like ordering off a restaurant menu. Of course, if you head into a French restaurant, and you don't speak French, it's a little tough. You're going to have a language barrier. And for most folks, it's the same problem with investments. You just don't know the language.

If your company has stock for sale, they may allow you to put a portion of your retirement in company stock. Many companies will match contributions with company stock. This may be a good deal, especially if they offer the stock at a discount. Your company may limit how much you can put into company stock. This change came after WorldCom and Enron, when employees had large amounts in company stock.[7] When the companies cratered, so did those retirement plans.

---

7 "Best practices for preventing 401(k) plan lawsuits" by Buckmann.

Having company stock within a retirement plan is not a bad thing. You just need to be careful. I'd recommend limiting the company stock portion to 20% or less. Diversify within the account by adding in other investments on the menu. I guess it's like aiming for a balanced diet. Steak is great, but if it's all you eat, you're probably malnourished.

TALKING POINT

If you don't know how to choose investments in your 401(k), get paid help. It's worth it.

Also, be careful about holding on to company stock after you leave the company. As long as you are an employee, you're an insider. Pay attention to sales and hiring. How is morale at the company? Are there changes in management pending? An astute employee can see whether a company is healthy or not. If you're no longer working there, you are not on the inside track. It's probably a good idea to get rid of the stock, upon the end of your employment.

The idea behind a plan menu is to offer something for everyone. So, there will be very conservative things on the menu, like a money market fund. There will be very aggressive things on the menu, like an emerging markets fund. And there will be all kinds of in-between flavors. It's up to you to choose a combination that fits you.

Beyond company stock, the items on the menu will be mutual funds. I'll talk about these investments in a chapter by themselves, so you'll need to read this before making those choices. For now, I'd like to discuss some general ideas.

First, know that we humans are strange creatures. And we

know that academics like to study our behavior and produce reams of paper to describe what we do. From research, we know that employees choose either 3 or 4 funds in their retirement plans. It doesn't really matter which 3 or 4. I guess after that number our eyes just glaze over. Maybe it's our short attention span. If we choose 4 funds, we allocate the contributions as follows: Fund A, 25%; Fund B, 25%; Fund C, 25%; Fund D, 25%.[8] We're no mathematical geniuses. Just keep it simple!

There's a fancy name for this. It's called heuristic allocation. Okay, so what happens when we choose 3 funds? Again, math is not our strong suit. We split the contribution evenly for 2 of the funds, and use the leftover amount to plug the third fund. So, we may allocate 3 funds as follows: Fund A, 30%, Fund B, 30%, and Fund C, 40%.[9] We're pretty simple creatures.

The problem with this is that we don't actually know what each fund is investing in. We simply go down the list 1, 2, 3, and 4 (OR 1, 2, and 3). It's like ordering in the French restaurant without knowing French. We choose based on what sounds good and find ourselves surprised when the dish arrives with 4 different versions of snails!

You want to create a balanced meal within your retirement plan. While a total of 3 or 4 funds in one retirement account is a good number, you need to choose a combination that makes sense for you. This should be based on your age, your personal preferences, and the amount accumulated in the account.

If you're just starting to work for a new company and you'll only be putting in $50 a month, you may not want to slice it

---

8 "Naïve Diversification Strategies in Defined Contribution Saving Plans" by Benartzi and Thaler.
9 *ibid.*

into 3 or 4 pieces. Choose just one, good fund. With a mutual fund, you're getting a group of investments, so don't be concerned about balancing at this point. All your money will go into one fund, and it will be easier to monitor. Later, as your account grows, you can choose more funds from the menu. A good rule of thumb is to add a fund at every $5000 mark until you have a total of four funds in the account.

Your age is an important consideration. If this is your first job at age 22, you can afford to be aggressive. You won't be touching this money until retirement, so you can withstand the ups and downs of the stock market. Look for good stock funds. With 4 funds, you should have a combination that represents big U.S. companies, small companies, and foreign companies. You probably won't think about adding bonds to your mix until you hit your 30s or 40s.

As you begin nearing retirement, you'll tone down your exposure to the stock market. If you're 62 and plan on retiring next year, you probably don't need to be all in stock funds. You also don't need to be all in bond funds. Remember, this is retirement money. Chances are that you won't withdraw EVERYTHING at retirement. Instead, this money is meant to last your lifetime. You need to make sure it can support you from retirement to grave. That means you probably need to keep some portion in stock funds. A good rule of thumb for those facing retirement is a 50/50 split between bond and stock funds.

Your personal preference is important, too. I've met 20 year olds who are afraid of the stock market, and I've met 80 year olds who want nothing BUT stock. The rule of thumb has to do with sleep. Yes, sleep. What combination lets you sleep at night? If it's keeping you awake, it's not worth it. Recognize that the returns on those funds are linked to risk. If you can't stand the risk, you are foregoing some return. But it may be worth it to you to sacrifice a few dollars for a few ZZZs!

Many mutual funds in retirement plans are available to the public, so you can find information on them at www.morningstar.com. Private funds should provide performance numbers and descriptions. Do some research before you make your selection. If your eyes are still rolling back in your head, pay an independent advisor for some help. It will be worth it to get it right on the front end.

The Value Meal of Retirement

If trying to put together a balanced meal within your retirement account is ust too much for you, you may want to go with a value meal. Value meals in retirement plans are balanced funds. They contain stocks, bonds, cash, plus other investments. You just need to order fund number 1 or 2 or 3, and you'll get everything you need.

Note I said OR. When you order a value meal at Wendy's, you don't also order fries and a drink to go with it. You know that the meal comes WITH fries and a drink. It's all inclusive. Balanced funds are all inclusive. If you choose one of these, resist your human nature! Don't add in 2 or 3 other funds just to round things out. ONE fund is all you need. It will provide you with good diversification across all types of investments.

Balanced funds may have the word "balanced" in their name. They may be called "asset allocation" funds. Find out what they are investing in. If they have a mix of bonds and stocks, they will (technically) be a balanced fund.

TALKING POINT

If you're clueless about investment options, choose the Life Cycle fund— but don't choose anything else!

Another type of balanced fund that is often on retirement plan menus is called a lifecycle fund. The Tax Relief Act of 2006 included some provisions to help with retirement planning. First, employers can automatically start deducting contributions from our paychecks for retirement. We must opt out versus opting in. Employers can also put this money into lifecycle funds versus leaving it in a low-paying money market fund.[10]

Lifecycle funds may be called "target" funds or may have a date attached. Their design is based on our age. If you are 30 years old and plan to retire around age 65, you might choose a fund called Target 2045. These funds automatically rebalance as you age and are a good choice, if you need something really simple. They are a collection of other mutual funds, so you only need this ONE fund. I'm amazed at the number of people who have 3 or 4 funds in their allocation, and one is a lifecycle fund!

If you go the lifecycle route, you will only have ONE fund. Again, resist the urge to throw in a few more choices. You don't need them. Choose a combination of funds from your employer plan menu that makes sense for you. Don't load up on steak and forget the veggies. If you want to create your own balance, choose 3 or 4 DIFFERENT funds. Keep your own tastes in mind

---

10 www.house.gov.

by picking a group that lets you sleep at night. If you decide to go the balanced or lifecycle route, remember, ONE fund.

How Often Should You Change Your Investments?

Technology has allowed us to have 24-7 access to our retirement accounts. That can be a bad thing, if you're constantly tinkering with your plan and obsessing over every dollar decline. It's retirement money and should be designed for your long-term use. I suggest seriously looking at this account twice a year, unless there is some change in your situation. Monitor the funds to see if they are performing as they should. Again, if this is out of your league, talk to a professional.

Plan on rebalancing once a year. You may have decided to keep 40% in bond funds and 60% in stock funds. Even if you don't want to change your mix, the account may have changed. Your stock funds may be growing, so that your allotted 60% is now 70% of your account. You'll need to slice off 10% that is in stock funds and move it to bond funds. Rebalance your existing account to get everything back in line. Next, you may want to change the allocation because you're getting closer to retirement or because you're not sleeping at night. With this, you'll need to rebalance your new contributions.

I often see people changing their allocations on contributions but forgetting to change the mix on the investments they've already accumulated. Keeping it simple means changing both sides so that they match. This will make it easier to track.

Lastly, look carefully at each statement you receive. Employers make mistakes. Plan administrators make mistakes. I can't tell you the number of times I've found errors on retirement accounts. Make sure the amounts deducted on your paycheck match what is going in the account. Understand that there will be a slight lag, since the money deducted today won't be sent in till later. Make sure the matching contribution is correct. Finally, make sure your allocations are up to date.

> ## TALKING POINT
>
> Evaluate your retirement accounts the same time each year, then forget about it.

Mainly, your job is to keep working and contributing to that plan. A little due diligence on investment choices means your money will be working hard for you. If you're not comfortable doing this, get help. Your retirement savings is too important to let this slide. Make a little effort on the front-end. Look at your statements a few minutes a quarter. Spend half an hour every six months evaluating the funds. Rebalance once a year. Gradually increase your contribution rate until you hit the maximum. While it really IS that important, it's NOT that difficult. But you have to make it a priority!

What Happens When You Change Jobs?

Gone are the days when you would retire from the company where you began your career. These days, employees are changing employers more often. That means you have bits and pieces of retirement floating around. The paperwork alone would drive me crazy! You might have quarterly statements coming from 3 different plans. And what happens when you move and forget to get your address changed? Will you just forget about that old account?

Again, I like simple. When you leave a job, you clean out your desk and take your personal stuff with you. You need to do the same with your retirement account. There are a couple of ways to do this.

First, check with your new employer and see if they will allow you to move the money from the previous plan to them. Not all plans allow for this, but some do. You'll have to talk to the administrators on both plans to find out how to do this. Some require that you complete a set of forms. Some will let you do it over the phone. If the forms look like Greek, get help. Most of the time, they send you a stack of paper, but you really only need to fill out a page or two.

If your new plan doesn't allow for this or you decide the new plan doesn't offer the best choices, you could move the money to an IRA account. This is called a rollover.[11] You are rolling over money from an employer retirement plan to an Individual Retirement Account. To do this, you need to open an IRA account.

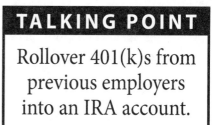

TALKING POINT

Rollover 401(k)s from previous employers into an IRA account.

You can do this at the bank, at a mutual fund, or at a brokerage house. As soon as you have an account number, you can tell the old plan (by phone or form), and they will send the money to the new account. In some cases, they will send the check to you, but it won't be made payable to you directly.

---

11 IRS Publication 590.

Moving old plan money to your new employer plan or moving it to an IRA account keeps your hands off the cash. This is moving retirement money (that has never been taxed) from one institution to another institution. If the IRS knows you won't be touching the cash, they're cool with it. This is the best way to move around retirement funds.

But if the IRS thinks you'll have access to the funds, they insist on taking their cut off the top. If your old plan distributes the money directly to you, they are required to send 20% of the total amount to the IRS. If you have $10,000 in a retirement plan and ask for a straight distribution, you'll only get a check for $8,000. That's $10,000 less a 10% penalty for early withdrawal and a 10% tax. If you turn around and put only $8,000 back in a retirement account, you're still short $2,000. That amount will be considered a distribution.

Some plans automatically send out checks on small accounts, when employees leave. Don't let this happen. You'll lose money, because of the taxes and penalties, even if you put the proceeds back into a retirement plan. Fill out the forms to allow the money to go from one institution to another institution. If you get a check made payable directly to you, don't cash it. Send it back to the administrator and ask that this be rolled over to an IRA or to a new plan.

If you want to roll over an old plan to a Fidelity mutual fund, for instance, you may receive a check made payable to: Fidelity, FBO Sally Jones. "FBO" stands for "For the Benefit Of." That's okay. Your name is on the check, but you won't be able to cash it. If you can cash it, though, you may be facing penalties and taxes.

When you change jobs, you want to move your retirement, as well. Consolidating your retirement savings helps you monitor and manage your funds. Be careful, though. Use the "roll-over" provision to move money from one institution to another institution. If you can't figure out how to do this, get professional help. Don't allow the money to come directly to you. And for goodness sake, don't think it's time to go shopping! You're going to need every penny you can get your hands on when you hit 65.

Vesting

Every industry has its own jargon and set of words. Vesting is one of those odd words often seen in retirement plans. Basically, it means ownership. If your employer offers a matching contribution, they may also have a vesting schedule. They entice you to participate in the plan with the match, but they hold a penalty over your head, if you leave them. They "own" the match until you have put in your time with them. Most have about a five year schedule, with gradual declines in the penalty.

A vesting schedule may look like this…

Year 1	80%
Year 2	60%
Year 3	40%
Year 4	20%
Year 5	0%

Remember, this schedule ONLY applies to the matching contributions. No one can take away money you put in from your paycheck. This is the way it works. If you leave the company before you've completed a year of employment, you'll lose 80% of the match. If you leave after three years but before four years, you'll lose 40% of the match. After five years of employment, you are fully vested. If you leave after five years, there is no penalty. All the money is yours to take with you.

Suppose you have $20,000 in a 401(k). Of that amount, $5,000 came from employer matching contributions. You've been with the company for three years. If you leave, you'll lose $2,000 (40% times $5,000), but you'll take $18,000 with you.

Employers set up vesting schedules to get you to stick around. Don't let this keep you from participating in a plan. Remember, YOUR contributions are never subject to a penalty. Also, don't let the vesting schedule keep you at a rotten job or keep you from a great opportunity. It's only one consideration.

IRAs

IRA stands for Individual Retirement Account. The "I" means there can only be one name on the account. Congress set up these accounts to give us another avenue to save for retirement. In particular, they can be used for people who don't have an employer plan. In many cases, though, you can use IRA accounts in ADDITION to your employer plan.

Currently, the most you can put in any IRA in a year is $5,000. If you are 50 or older, you have a catch-up contribution of $1,000, so your annual total is $6,000. Occasionally, they adjust these maximum amounts. The IRS doesn't care how many accounts you use, or the types of IRAs you use, as long as you don't go over the maximum amount. If you are 35, you can put $50 into 100 different IRA accounts ($50 x 100

= $5,000). Please don't, though. You'll just be complicating your life.

And, while $5,000 is the maximum for a 35 year old, that doesn't mean you have to put in $5,000. You can put in $50 or $500 or $2,500. It doesn't matter, just so long as you don't go over the annual amount. So, just do something!

IRAs are designed for retirement, so the plan is to leave the money alone until you stop working. In fact, there is a penalty for taking money out before you are 59½.[12] Don't ask me why they decided on the "½." If you take money out before this magic age, there is a 10% penalty. If you take out $1000, you'll pay an extra $100 to the IRS in penalty fees.

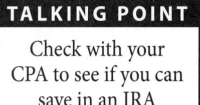

TALKING POINT

Check with your CPA to see if you can save in an IRA account, in addition to your 401(k).

The 59½ rule often causes 20 year olds to avoid IRA accounts. They can't imagine 30, much less 59½. Knowing this, Congress gave us a few exceptions to the penalty. You can take money out of an IRA account penalty-free for the first time purchase of a home up to $10,000. Just knowing this is a possibility will often nudge younger people to use IRAs to save.

Another exception involves education. If you use the money for educational purposes, there is no penalty. It doesn't have to be for YOUR education. You can use the money for your child's education, making this a great way to save for your child's col-

---

12 IRS Publication 590.

lege. There are additional exceptions involving healthcare or disability.[13] Check with your CPA on these.

With IRA accounts, that 10% penalty may not be the only thing reducing your $1000 withdrawal. You may also have to pay tax on the amount you take out. This depends on the type of IRA you have and on how long you've had the account.[14]

Traditional IRAs

There are 2 types of IRAs. One is called a Traditional IRA. It works just like your 401(k). The money going into the account is not taxed. With your employer plan, the contributions to your 401(k) come out of your paycheck before the federal income tax is calculated. That means a dollar that goes into your 401(k) may only be about seventy cents less on your paycheck (depending on your tax bracket).

If you put money into a Traditional IRA, you are writing the check out of your savings or checking account. Since you've already paid tax on this money, you can take a deduction on your income taxes in the year you make the contribution. If you make $35,000 a year, and you put $5,000 into your IRA account(s), you will only show $30,000 on your income tax form. Your tax bracket determines your savings. If you are in the 15% tax bracket, saving $5,000 in an IRA account will SAVE you $750 on your tax bill. If you're in the 28% tax bracket, the savings is $1,400!

Not everyone qualifies for the tax deduction on a Traditional IRA. You must fit into certain income brackets. These depend

---

13 IRS Publication 590.
14 IRS Publication 590.

on your marital status, and the brackets are adjusted regularly. Check with your CPA to see if you qualify. You may also qualify, if you don't have access to a retirement plan at work. Here's the catch on Traditional IRAs. When you get ready to take the money out, you will pay income tax on every penny you withdraw. We get a tax break when we put the money in, but the taxes are only deferred. That means you won't pay now, but you'll pay later. If you are 60 years old (no penalty here) and take out $1,000, you will show an extra $1,000 of income on your tax form. Now, if you're tax bracket is 15%, that $1,000 will COST you $750.

So, you're now saying this looks like a wash. You get a $750 savings up front, only to pay it back later. Well, it's not quite a wash. First, the idea is that you may have a lower tax bracket in retirement than what you had while you were working. You may end up with a $1,400 tax break at age 35 and a $750 tax bill at age 60. Of course, you could end up with the opposite relationship. And, don't forget the time value of money. $750 now is worth more than $750 twenty-five years from now.

One other thing, earnings on your IRA account are not taxed from year to year.[15] Dividends, interest, and capital gains are not reported on IRA accounts. This allows your $1,000 contribution to grow unfettered by a tax bill. You can trade as much as you want in an IRA account without worrying about short-term versus long-term gains. You NEVER want to put municipal bonds in an IRA account, since you don't pay tax on bond interest. You can "play" in this account as much as you dare without worrying about the tax bill at the end of the year.

That brings us back to the penalties. If you take money out of your Traditional IRA account before age 59 ½, you may have

---

15 IRS Publication 590.

to pay the 10% penalty AND the taxes due on the withdrawal. That $1,000 withdrawal will cost you $100 in a penalty. If your tax bracket is 28%, the tax will be $280 ($1,000 x 0.28). Your total bill for this short-sighted folly will be $380. Ouch! Even if you use one of the IRS exceptions and avoid the penalty, you'll still have to pay tax based on your income tax bracket. Hopefully, this will make you think twice about raiding your IRA account.

While Congress wanted us to keep our mitts off this money until retirement, they eventually wanted to get some tax revenue out of us. So, at age 70½ (again with the ½), you MUST start taking money out of your Traditional IRA account. The amount you take out is not penalized, because you are over that magic age of 59½. Now, you are penalized if you DON'T take out the proper amount. In fact, the penalty is in the 50% neighborhood.[16] Gulp! RMD is the Required Minimum Distribution and is a calculation based on the value of your account and on your age. Your financial advisor should be able to help you with this.

Roth IRAs

The other type of IRA is called a Roth IRA. It is named for the senator who sponsored the bill to create these accounts. The 59½ rule applies to this type of IRA. The same exceptions apply. The annual maximums and the catch-up contribution for those over 50 are the same.

The big difference is the tax deduction. With a Roth IRA, you don't get a tax break for money you put into the account.

---

16 IRS Publication 590.

If you put $1,000 into a Roth IRA, it doesn't help you one bit with your tax bill. So, why do it?

Here's the big carrot on Roth accounts...

Earnings on Roth IRAs are tax-free! That's right. They're tax-free, NOT tax-deferred. When you take out $1,000 at age 60, there is no tax bill. Because the IRS got their payment up front, they don't expect any taxes on the back end. It's a beautiful thing!

There are also income limits on Roth IRAs, but they're higher than Traditional IRAs. Check with your CPA to see if you qualify. Another difference with Roth IRAs is that there is no RMD.[17] When you hit 70½, you are not required to take out any money. This allows you to pass on more money to your heirs, if you choose.

One thing you should know: there is a five year rule with Roth IRAs. You must leave the money in for five years to get the tax-free carrot.

Which IRA to Use?

So, which IRA should you use? That depends. Generally, I encourage young people to use Roth IRAs. The time they have until retirement makes the tax-free status more valuable. All those years of earnings piling up on top of each other without tax is priceless (well, almost). Of course, young families are often struggling to cover today's bills. They may need to use a Traditional IRA just to lower their tax bill. And folks already near retirement may not have five years to keep money in a Roth account, so they may opt for a Traditional IRA.

---

17 IRS Publication 590.

Roths are my first choice, but your particular situation may lead you to choose the Traditional IRA. I'm going to sound like a broken record, but check with your CPA or financial advisor. He or she will advise you on the best option for you and your family.

What About Small Businesses?

Small businesses need retirement plans, too! But setting up and administering 401(k) s can be expensive. That's why Congress created some tools for small business owners that keep the costs down but allow for retirement savings beyond the IRA amounts.

SEP IRAs

One is called a SEP IRA. SEP stands for Simplified Employee Pension account. They are IRAs, so the same rules apply. There are penalties for withdrawals under the age of 59 ½, but you also have a set of exceptions to the early withdrawal penalty. They are tax-deferred, so the money going in to SEPs are not taxed, only the money coming out (hopefully, when you're retired). In this way, they function just like Traditional IRA accounts.[18]

The one big difference is in the annual maximum contribution. You can put up to 25% of your income into a SEP IRA each year. Dollar-wise, you can't go above $49,000 this year.[19] So, 25% or $49,000, whichever is larger. The percentage is ad-

---

18 IRS Publication 560.
19 *ibid*.

justed downward if you are listed as self-employed. This big allowance lets you sock away a lot of money into retirement accounts. It also allows you to protect a lot of income from Uncle Sam.

If you have a consulting business, and you make $100,000 during the year, you can put $25,000 into your SEP IRA account. That means you will pay federal income tax on only $75,000. This is definitely a case of paying yourself before you pay Uncle Sam.

SEP IRAs are ideal for one person businesses. All contributions come from the employer, so if you're both the owner and the employee, you want to put away as much as possible. Each year, you choose the percentage of your income to put into your SEP. Some years, you may only be able to put in 10%, and other years you'll be able to put in the entire 25%. Some years, you may not be able to contribute at all. It just depends on the cash you have on hand.

TALKING POINT

Don't forget that "business on the side." You can set up a retirement account that will cut your tax bill.

The downside of SEP IRAs is that this decision gets complicated when you have employees. Whatever percentage you apply to YOUR salary is the same you'll apply to each and every employee. The law allows some limitations, such as only including employees who have been with you for three years, but you can't cut out employees indiscriminately. Any employee with at least $450 in earnings qualifies for an employer contribution, so you're going to be contributing to part-time employees' plans. Whatever percentage you apply to your salary must also be applied to each of their salaries. And that's where it gets expensive.[20]

SEP IRAs can be used for businesses with up to 25 employees, but I usually tell business owners to think twice about these plans if they have ANY employees. There is no vesting plan with SEP IRAs. The minute the money goes in, it's theirs. You may put money into your employee's account today, and they leave tomorrow. Your money is gone. So, if your business is just YOU, a SEP IRA is the way to go. If you have a one-man shop or a business on the side, SEP IRAs allow you to accumulate retirement savings and help with the tax bill.

Any place that allows you to open IRA accounts will also allow you to open SEP IRAs. There are a few more pieces of paper to sign. You'll have a document with a few boxes checked that declare how the plan will work. Each employee will have a separate account. Your investments will be limited only by the institution where you opened the account.

SIMPLE IRAs

If you have 100 employees or less, you can use another small business plan called a SIMPLE IRA. This stands for Savings Incentive Match Plan for Employees.

SIMPLE IRAs are salary deferral plans. That means each employee can decide to contribute or not. Employers can match contributions dollar for dollar up to 3%, or employers can put in 2% for every employee, regardless of their contributions.[21]

---

20 IRS Publication 560.
21 *ibid.*

Most choose the 3% route, because this encourages employees to put in their own dollars. If they don't contribute, you don't have to put in a dime. Like SEPs, vesting is 100% and immediate. That means the minute the money goes in, it's theirs. The same IRA rules apply. The annual contribution on SIMPLEs is less than SEP accounts. The annual deferral limit for this year is $11,500. The catch-up contribution for people who are 50 or over is $2,500. So, if I'm 50 or over (I know this is a stretch!), then I can contribute a total of $14,000 to my SIMPLE IRA this year.[22] This amount is adjusted from time to time.

Most small businesses can't afford to put in large amounts into retirement plans, but they want to offer employees a way to save. A SIMPLE is the way to go. You can open these accounts at many of the same places as IRAs. Again, you have a few more forms to complete, but it's not much. Each employee will have his own account. The investment choices are limited only by the institution you choose.

By law, you can limit participation to employees who have been with you for two years and to those who have made at least $5,000 in the last two calendar years. The broader income limits and the matching option make this plan appealing to business owners with employees.

SIMPLE IRAs and SEP IRAs are designed for small businesses who can't afford to start 401(k) plans. They are easy to open. There are no annual tax filings. The cost to administer is minor. Which option you choose depends on your particular business and your set of employees. But by all means, make use of these plans to save for retirement and shelter income.

---

22 IRS Publications 560.

Stacking Plans

One more thing, you may be able to stack plans. Just because you have a 401(k) or a SIMPLE IRA or a SEP IRA doesn't mean you can't also have a Roth IRA or Traditional IRA. Depending on your income limits, you may be able to do both. Check with your CPA. When it comes to retirement, you need to use every avenue available to prepare.

CHAPTER NINE

Talking about Investing

Investing can be an intimidating experience. For some, it feels like putting money on a number on the roulette wheel. And if you invest like you bet in the casino (on a whim and a prayer), it can be. If it's done right, it's a way to put your money to work for you.

I often say, "If you can read, you can invest." But most people don't bother to read before they put their money down. When it comes to their 401(k), they simply choose the funds their office mate recommends, or they try an adult form of eeny, meeny, miny, mo. When it comes to investing in individual stocks, they depend on hot tips from their plumber or their cousin. Even with your basic savings account, they just use the local bank their grandfather used.

Real investing takes effort. First, you must educate yourself about the world of investments. You must research particular investments to see if the idea is sound. Then you must navigate the world of financial services to figure out how to buy what you want. It's not easy, but it's really NOT that difficult.

Investing, like other worthwhile ventures, takes practice. Expect to fail occasionally. In fact, the failures may teach you more than the successes. Know that there are many people out there also trying to win at this game. Don't

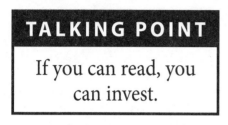

TALKING POINT

If you can read, you can invest.

think you have some silver bullet. No one does. Those newsletter or television gurus? Believe me. If their methods were as foolproof as they claim, they wouldn't need you to buy their newsletter or tune into their program.

Investing has taught me more about humility than anything else I've tried. Just when you think you've got it all figured out, you get knocked on your tail. Theory and history teach us about markets, but they don't tell us a blooming thing about what's going to happen tomorrow. Hopefully, learning theory and history keeps us grounded when things go crazy. And they will.

Ultimately, this dicey game of investing in financial markets boils down to human beings. And those creatures can be annoyingly predictable or absurdly chaotic. You never know which you'll get. For the investor, the trick is to keep your emotions AND your ego out of the transaction. Remember, it's all about making money.

A Primer on Financial Markets

When you invest, you step into the world of financial markets. A financial market is like any other market. There is a buyer and a seller. Once they find each other, the buyer will pay some premium for what the seller has to offer.

Suppose I go to a fish market. I'm hungry, and I want fish. I have no fish. In the market, some vendors have too much fish, more fish than they or their family can consume. So I need fish. I'm the buyer. The vendor with too much fish is the seller.

The fish market is the clearinghouse. It's the place where people with too much fish set up tables and signs to sell their fish. It's the place I'll go to find the fish I need. Maybe I stop at the first table I see and buy my fish. Maybe I search through all the vendors for the freshest fish at the best price. Maybe the vendor with the largest table and the jugglers out front gets my business.

However it happens, the buyer and seller must find each other. Now, the seller isn't going to just give me that fish. I have to exchange something for it. For most exchanges, the medium is money. We agree on a price. I pay the seller of fish. He gives me the fish. We both go away happy. That's how a market works.

Financial markets function the same way. What you need to understand is that, in financial markets, you're not buying or selling fish. You're buying or selling money. That's right. Money.

If I have a good business idea, but I need money to start my business, I go to the financial markets. I don't have enough money, so I am the buyer. Some people have too much money (I know. I know. WHO has too much money?). They are the sellers.

The buyers and sellers have to find each other. They may do this through a formal market, like out stock exchange, or they may do this through a private set of meetings, like a private placement. Regardless, the two parties have to get together.

Once they get together, they must agree on a price. The price of money is interest. If I "buy" $20,000 for a new car, I'll have to pay back more than $20,000. The difference between the loan and the payback amount is interest, or the price of money. Interest rates or returns on investments are quoted in percentage terms. Think of those terms as the price tag for the money. It's how you shop in the "money markets."

If you have an extra $5,000 in your bank account, and you open a CD, you are selling your money to the bank. They buy your money and use it to make more money. Then, they will pay you back the $5,000 plus interest. You find each other by seeing an ad in the paper or a banner in the bank or by having your banker make you an offer.

If you have $5,000 to buy stock, and you decide to buy shares in an Initial Public Offering (IPO), you are selling your money. This is a company that needs extra cash to expand their business. You have extra cash. You get together. You may be buying stock, but in the financial marketplace, you are actually the seller. The company issuing the stock is the buyer of your money. You hope that your payback will be greater than your initial investment, but, in this case, there is no guarantee. You are taking a bigger chance with your money than with the CD, so you expect a bigger pay-off.

The greater the risk associated with the transaction, the higher the price tag. It's what we call the risk-reward tradeoff. Guaranteed returns, generally, will be lower than those for investments that are anybody's guess.

Everything that makes it a better deal for the buyer of money means the price goes up. You want to use the money for 20 years versus one year? That'll cost you in a higher interest rate. You want to be able to renegotiate the deal later? That'll cost you. You want me to take a chance on a brand new idea? That'll cost you.

Everything that makes it a better deal for the seller of money means the price goes down. You want me to put up collateral for the loan? You'll have to lower the price. You want me to let you take back the money any time? Lower the price. You want a guarantee? Lower the price.

When you are the seller in a financial market, you must be choosy. You are selling your extra cash, and you want to get the most for it. Investing a portfolio is like running a business. You're always trying to increase your profit margin, just like the fish vendor, without getting too crazy or too greedy.

In a local fish market, you may expect to see a few hundred customers come through. With globalization and technology, the number of customers in financial markets increases dramatically. For the seller of money (the investor), there are thousands of options for investing that money. Learning how to access the best corners and how to negotiate the best prices may mean the difference in a comfortable retirement and a stellar one. That's where education and research pay off.

Types of Investments

Basically, there are two ways to invest. You can either be an owner, or you can be a lender. If you loan someone money, you expect to receive interest plus the loan amount back at some specified time. You may get less than this, if the borrower defaults, but you will never get any more than this. If you become an owner, all bets are off. There is no specified payoff date. There is no specified payoff amount. There is no set interest payment. Your loss could be 100%, but it could also be limitless.

Typically, owning is riskier than lending, but it can also be more rewarding. If you own an entire piece of property and you

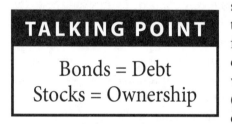

TALKING POINT

Bonds = Debt
Stocks = Ownership

sell it for $10,000 more than you paid for it, that full gain is yours. If you own the property equally with your brother-in-law (never a good idea), you only gain $5,000. Your gain or your loss depends on your proportional ownership.

Most investors do a bit of both: owning and lending. Putting the two together gives you the best of both worlds. The lending investments give you a set income and a set return. If you're careful about who you lend to, you should get your principal back. Ownership investments allow for the possibility of greater gains, as you participate in the growth of the underlying asset.

Lenders

So, how do you lend money in financial markets?

You lend money when you buy any type of bond. Bonds are debt instruments. You may also hear them called fixed-income instruments. That's because the payments are "fixed" in some way. When you go to the bank to get a car loan, there is a contract to sign. In the contract, there are terms of the loan: interest rate, payoff date, early payment terms. With each bond issue, there is a contract that specifies how the loan will work.

While we tend to think of bonds as dull and ordinary, they are really quite complex. Each issue is different. Each type of bond works differently. And there are constantly evolving ways of packaging these loans. Loan contracts may have a lot of bells and whistles attached. If you are the lender, you want to make sure these work in your favor.

When you ask for a car loan from the bank, their utmost concern is that you'll pay them back. It's the same when you buy any type of bond. You are loaning someONE or some institution money. The best thing you can do is make sure they have any income to cover their debt payments. Of course, if you buy a 10 year bond, it may be difficult to figure out if your borrower will still be a good risk 10 years from now.

Sometimes, bonds are just called bonds. When corporations issue them, they are called corporate bonds. When cities issue them, they are called municipal bonds. CDs are, basically, bonds. You are loaning money to a bank. Treasuries are bonds. You are loaning money to the U.S. government (please do, they need it right now). Collateralized Mortgage Obligations (CMOs) are special types of bonds that are backed by mortgages. Fannie Maes and Freddie Macs are also special types of mortgage bonds. Short-term commercial paper is a lending instrument.

Bonds come in many shapes and sizes. When you buy a bond, first determine whom you are loaning money TO. Are they a good risk? Then find out how long the loan will last. Will they be a good risk for the duration of the loan? What interest rate will they pay you? Can they pay off the loan early? What happens if they can't make the payments? Are there other provisions in the loan that could be a problem for you?

What if you get in a cash crunch and need your money back sooner than the payoff date? CDs issued by local banks are not usually traded. If you need your money back before the maturity date, you'll pay a penalty. Most bonds can be traded, though. When you sell your bond, the borrower is not paying you off early. Instead, you are selling the bond to some other lender. They will continue the loan until its maturity date. How quickly you can sell a bond and the price you get for it depend on the borrower's reputation, the particular bond, and the current interest rate.

All in all, being a lender can be a good thing. You'll get steady income from the debt payments, and you'll get back the money you loaned. Bonds are great for folks who need income to live on. They are perfect for retired investors who are living off their portfolio. They tend to be steady, stodgy earners. Don't expect to hit the jackpot with bonds, but if you like stability, they may be just right for you.

Owners

Owning is easier to figure out. When you buy stock, you become part owner in a business. With most public corporations, though, there are tens of thousands of other owners. You only own a small portion of the company, but you're still an owner. If the company invents a new video game that every teenager has to have, you should see the value of your shares go up. Your piece of the company is only as good as the company itself.

Your fortunes fall and rise with the fortunes of the company. That means you need to do your homework. What have they earned in the past? How do their sales look? Will the recession hurt the company? Is their manager any good? What can you expect their sales and earnings to be in the future? Are they selling gas guzzlers when everyone wants electric cars?

Buying stock is both science and art. The science comes in when you analyze a company's financial statements and study their competitors. Look at the numbers from every angle. Read every footnote in the financial statements for anything shady. Apply every financial ratio you can think of.

Then, comes the art, because you must gaze into the crystal ball. What will their business be like tomorrow or next year? Will their products even be in demand? Will they be able to navigate through their field of competitors? Will some unforeseen event, like an earthquake or a hurricane or a terrorist attack, derail their business? After all the research, the decision to buy stock is a leap of faith.

There are two ways to earn money on stocks. The first is through dividend payments. Not all companies pay dividends, though. Younger companies don't usually pay dividends because they are holding on to every dollar for investment in the company. Older, more established companies usually pay dividends.

Most dividends are paid on a quarterly basis, so four times a year you should receive a payment. The dividend is announced on a per share basis and is decided by the board of directors of the company. If the dividend is $0.10 per share and you own 100 shares, you'll receive $10.00. You can use your cash to go to lunch, or you can use it to invest.

Many companies allow shareholders to buy more shares

with each dividend payment. This is called a DRIP-- Dividend Reinvestment Plan. Unless you need the cash to live on, I recommend reinvesting the cash dividends in more shares. It's a great way to build a stock position.

The average dividend payment for stocks in the S&P 500 (big U.S. companies) is only about 2%, so for owners, this steady income stream represents only a small portion of your return. The other part comes from the increase in the share price. This is called the capital gain. If you buy 100 shares for $10.00 per share and sell the shares for $15.00 per share, your gain is $500 or $5.00 per share.

Remember, though, that this gain could just as easily be a loss. That's the risk of being an owner. Stock prices go both ways. Hopefully, you have chosen a company with good prospects. If that's the case and IF you give it enough time, you'll see a payoff. Stock ownership can come with big rewards, but they also come with big risks.

If the company you buy doesn't pay a dividend, you are banking on your entire return coming from a capital gain. That makes it even riskier. Ownership requires thoughtful analysis before the purchase and a great deal of patience after purchase. Big, quick payoffs happen, but they're not the norm. That means you should never use your short-term money to buy shares of stock.

If you purchase shares in an IPO (Initial Public Offering), you are buying shares directly from the company. They will take your money and use it to "grow" the company. Most of the time, though, you are buying shares from another investor. Remember, each time you buy shares of a company convinced they are going up, you are buying from someone else who is equally convinced they are going down. It's a sobering thought.

Variations

There are many variations of lending and owning. Every day, someone on Wall Street is coming up with a new way to package lending or owning. Ultimately, each newfangled security is some form of loan or some form of ownership. In fact, one security can actually have qualities of both.

Mutual funds are pooled investments. That is, you pool or put your money in with other investors. The manager of the fund buys a group of securities. This group is the fund's portfolio. The portfolio may contain bonds. The portfolio may be all stocks. The portfolio could be gold, or real estate, or any other investment. The portfolio may even contain bonds, stocks, gold AND real estate.

When you buy shares of a mutual fund, you are saying that you want to invest in the securities that are in the portfolio. Don't buy a bond mutual fund if you want to own stocks and vice versa. Find out what the fund manager is buying. Are these the types of securities you want to buy? Is the manager any good at picking investments? How much will it cost to participate in the fund?

Morningstar is a mutual fund research company and has a great website for finding information on funds. You can find information on the fund's past performance, its holdings, and its expenses. Anyone investing in a 401(k) needs to research those fund choices.

Annuities are variations of lending and owning. They usually combine life insurance with investing. Fixed annuities allow you to invest in bond portfolios. They offer a fixed rate of interest, which is adjusted on some schedule. Variable annuities are like 401(k) s. There is a list of mutual funds in which you can invest. Some will be bond mutual funds. Some will be stock mutual funds. The choice is yours. That means, of course, that the risks and the rewards are also yours.

Be careful about investing in annuities. They usually have surrender charges that make them quite inflexible. They are often high commission products and often have high annual expenses. Make sure they fit your needs.

There are many other types of investments. Before you take the plunge, make sure you understand how each works. I'm not going into the world of derivatives here. These are short-term bets on the movement of some underlying asset. I usually advise individual investors to stay away from this game.

Off to Market to Buy a Fat Pig

So, you've picked your set of investments. Now, how do you actually buy that bond or the shares of stock?

For the standard bonds and stocks, you'll need to go through a brokerage house. You may choose to use a full-service broker or a discount broker.

With a full-service broker, you get more service. You would expect to receive advice and assistance on opening accounts and handling trades. Of course, you'll pay extra for this service. Merrill Lynch and Edward Jones are full-service brokers, for example.

If you want to handle things on your own, you may choose to use a discount broker. Schwab and T.D. Ameritrade are discount brokers, for example. You won't get advice, and you will probably handle your own paperwork and trading. The trade-off is that it will cost you much less to go this route.

Many brokerage houses also allow you to buy and sell a variety of mutual funds. You can also deal directly with the fund, though. You will simply open an account with Fidelity or Vanguard or whichever set of funds you want. Any time you want to make changes, you'll deal directly with the fund company. If you want to purchase an annuity, you'll probably need to consult with an insurance salesperson.

Now, you can open accounts online, transfer money online, trade online, and request funds online. With the internet, it's easy to open a brokerage account or mutual fund account. Just find their site, and fill in the blanks. You'll have to send in money to get the account going.

Remember, the more you are willing to do yourself, the less you will pay. If you need help, though, pick up the phone or head into a local investment office. The price you pay may be worth it. If you're investing in your 401(k), access is a matter of filling out paperwork with your employer. Making changes is often a matter of logging on to the investment site.

So, the actual buying and selling of investments is a piece of cake. The hard part comes before the trade. Do your homework. Understand what you're getting into. Pay attention to your investments, but don't obsess over them. Risk and reward are connected. Don't expect a high return on a guaranteed investment, and don't expect a guarantee on a high return investment.

CHAPTER TEN

Talking about Insurance

I hate insurance. I need it, but I hate it. When insurance salespeople start talking, it's like a sleeping pill. I feel myself nodding off. I want to shout, "Stop talking." Two sentences into their monologue, and I feel like I'm in a foreign country. I see their lips moving, but I haven't a clue what they're saying! So, don't expect me to talk a lot about this subject. It's not my favorite.

I think most people feel the same as I do. And I think it leads most of us to make poor decisions on insurance. Most people are over insured, and most are paying too much for their insurance.

First, use insurance to cover the "what ifs" in life-- what if I die; what if I become disabled; what if a tornado hits my house; what if I run over someone; what if I need nursing home care.

Don't use insurance as an investment. If a salesperson tries to talk you into something with an investment option, just say no. The add-ons will only cost you money.

Next, only use insurance for as long as you need it. You will probably always need house insurance or health insurance, but you may not always need life insurance. Life insurance is there to protect your family from the loss of your income. Don't buy life insurance for children. The death of a child is rare, and the funeral costs are not that high. If you have accumulated enough money to cover your family, you no longer need that life policy. If your children are grown, you may decide to drop your life policy. For most, a good term policy is usually the best option. The cost is low and provides you with maximum coverage only for the time you need it.

With insurance, your big concern is that the company will be there when you need them. Insurance is regulated by each state, so check with your local insurance commissioner about the health of the company. Check with family and friends about their personal experiences with a company. Did they pay off in a reasonable time? Was it easy to file a claim?

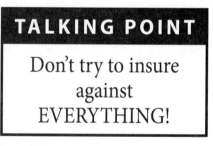

TALKING POINT

Don't try to insure against EVERYTHING!

Don't try to insure against EVERY possibility. You may get cancer, but you may not. A good, general health policy is your best bet. An earthquake MAY hit Mississippi, but it's more likely it won't. Use a good, general homeowner's policy. Aim for good value for your dollar on insurance. You don't want to be spending so much on insurance that you can't save. After all, your best protection against life's what ifs is a healthy savings account.

Each year, pull out those policies BEFORE the insurance guy shows up. When you add up all the premiums, does it make your eyes grow wide? Do you have enough insurance, or do you have too much? Could your money be better spent elsewhere? Before you let that salesperson in the door, know what you need to protect your family. Then, stand your ground, because you are getting VERY SLE-E-E-EPY!

Epilogue

Whew! I'm out of breath. I've talked and talked, and the conversation has just started. Up until this point, it's been a monologue. Now it's your turn.

This book has been a broad overview of the world of budgets and finance, but it's just a taste of each area. To try to explain every detail on each subject would have been overwhelming. I'm sure you would have tuned me out about halfway through! But you should have some idea about how this world works. Also, hopefully, you have some tools and tricks to navigate the complicated alleyways of finance.

If you want to concentrate on your family budget, spend time finding ways to address your family's issues. Learn more about budgeting by digging into the details. Pay attention to those credit card bills, and know your rights under the new law. Get on firm footing in this area before going on to the next item.

Then, you may want to become an expert on saving. Spend time on the internet looking for good savings rates and good options for your emergency money. Get comfortable with moving your money around to get the best rate. Learn to negotiate with your bank.

Check out the possibility for college savings within your state. Call the Treasurer's Office. Check out their website. Choose the best option for your children, and talk to family members about helping with this venture.

Finally, look at your investments. Start with your 401(k). Learn to read the statement. Research each option on the plan menu. Adjust your contributions to get the most out of your retirement savings. Know your contribution rate, and find ways to boost the number.

When you're ready for more advanced investing, consider a discount broker. Open an account. Build up cash for investing. Do your own homework, and don't rely on tips from your neighbor. There are many books out there on investing in stocks, bonds, and mutual funds. Find one that is written by someone with a good, long-term record. And, practice, practice, practice.

More than anything, look closely at the lessons you are passing on to your children. Are you setting them up for bad habits or equipping them for wealth building? Spend time talking to them about money and finance.

The world of money and finance is big and complicated, but it IS understandable. You just need to take a piece at the time. Learn the language. Understand how to calculate time value of money. Don't get carried away with the exotic stuff. Stick with the simple and tried and true.

Being able to "talk money" is like being able to speak French in Paris. You may be able to get around by guessing the signposts and depending on translators, but you won't really get where you want to go efficiently without knowing the language yourself.

ANYONE can be a good financial manager. It just takes a little time and effort. And it takes the confidence to jump into the conversation. So, keep talking, and keep asking questions. When times get tough, knowledge is power. A financial crisis may make you want to turn up the music and tune out all the bad news, but the real way to handle the fear is to get educated. When all is said and done, money talks. The question is, "Are you listening?"

Works Cited

"2008-09 College Prices." www.collegeboard.com. 27 Aug 2009. Web.

Benartzi, Shlomo, Richard H. Thaler. "Naive Diversification Strategies in Defined Contribution Savings Plans." *The American Economic Review* (2001): 79-80. Print.

Bishop, Ph. D., Paul C., Harika Bickicioglu and Shonda D. Hightower. "The 2006 National Association of Realtors Profile of Home Buyers and Sellers." National Association of Realtors (2007). 24 Aug 2009. Web.

Block, Sandra. "Companies rethink 401(k) matches." *USA Today*. 25 June 2009. Print.

Buckmann, Carol I. "Best practices for preventing 401(k) plan lawsuits." *Employee Benefit News*. 01 Mar 2008. 28 Aug 2009. Web.

"The Buzz." *Money*. May 2008: 14. Print.

Colquitt, L. Lee, V. Carlos Slawson, Jr.. "Understanding the Cost of Private Mortgage Insurance." www.westga.edu. 1997. 25 Aug 2009. Web.

"The Emergency Fund." [Weblog It's Your Money!]. 24 Aug 2009. Web. www.mdmproofing.com/iym/emergency_fund.shtml.

"FAQs: Fafsa on the Web." www.fafsa.ed.gov. 26 Aug 2009. Web.

Fareed, Zakaria. "Get Out the Wallets." *Newsweek*. 10 Aug 2009: 20. Print.

Garrett, Sheryl, Marie Swift. "Just Give Me the Answers: Expert Advisors Address Your Most Pressing Financial Questions." *Kaplan Business* (2004). Print.

McCourt, Stephen P.. "Defined Benefit and Defined Contribution Plans: A History, Market Overview and Comparative Analysis." *Benefits & Compensation Digest* (2006): 43. Print.

"Mortgage Rates in Jackson, MS." www.bankrate.com. 25 Aug 2009. Web.

"Numbers to Know for 2009." *Money*. Jan 2009: 17. Print.

Roberts, Dexter, and Chi-Chu Tschang. "China's Consumers: Too Scared to Spend." *BusinessWeek*. 08 Dec 2008: 62-63. Print.

"Senior Series: Facts About Retirement." www. ohioline.osu.edu/ss-fact/0200.html. The Ohio State University Extension. 28 Aug 2009. Web.

United States. Federal Reserve Board and the Office of Thrift Supervision. *A Consumer's Guide to Mortgage Refinancing*. GPO. Print.

United States. Internal Revenue Service. Publication 560. 2009. Print.

United States. Internal Revenue Service. Publication 575. 2009. Print

United States. Internal Revenue Service. Publication 590. 2009. Print.

United States. U.S. Congress. Credit Card Accountability, Responsibility, and Disclosure Act of 2009. www.house.gov. Web.

United States. U.S. Congress. The Tax Relief Act of 2006. www.house.gov. Web.

Weston, Liz Pulliam. "The truth about credit card debt." *MSN Money*. 30 April 2006. 24 Aug 2009. Web.

"What is a 529 Plan?." www.savingforcollege.com. 25 Aug 2009. Web.

"What is a VA Loan?." www.valoans.com. 25 Aug 2009. Web.

About the Author

Nancy Lottridge Anderson has been in the investment business for more than 20 years. For the past 15 years, she has run her own financial advisory business, New Perspectives, Inc., located in Ridgeland, Mississippi. Nancy has her Ph.D. in Business Administration with a concentration in Finance from Mississippi State University and is also an Assistant Professor of Finance at Mississippi College. In 1996, she received her designation as a Chartered Financial Analyst and has served as President of the CFA Society of Mississippi. Currently, she is the only woman in Mississippi holding both a CFA charter and a Ph.D. Nancy is co-host of the Mississippi Public Broadcasting radio show, *Money Talks*. She serves on the board for the Mississippi Council on Economic Education. Nancy lives with her husband in Clinton, Mississippi, where she waits patiently for grandchildren.